the Debut

Hey Vanessa!
Thanx for the
408 support, San Jose
& life.

the Debut
THE MAKING OF A FILIPINO AMERICAN FILM

Gene Cajayon and John Manal Castro
with Dawn Bohulano Mabalon

Vanessa!
Thanks 4 the CD!

Gene C

Tulitos Press
Filipino American Literature & Culture
Chicago & Santa Cruz ◇ 2001

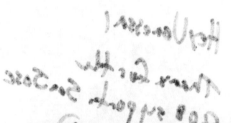

the Debut: The Making of a Filipino American Film
Gene Cajayon and John Manal Castro
with Dawn Bohulano Mabalon

Tulitos Press
Filipino American Literature & Culture
1507 E. 53rd Street / PMB #211 / Chicago, IL 60615
http://www.tulitospress.com/

Editorial	Jean Vengua Gier
Production	Elizabeth H. Pisares
Assistance	Matthew Aron, Nerissa Balce-Cortes, Oscar Peñaranda, and Fabio Rojas.
Advice	Catie Cariaga, Gary Colmenar, Julie Koo/Kaya Productions, Michael Roche, Marie Romero/Arkipelago Books, Steve Olko/Data Reproductions, Anatalio Ubalde, Jr., and indie-press@yahoogroups.com.

Cover and Insert Design	Rosa+Wesley
Cover and Insert Photography	Shane Sato
Cover Makeup	Nanette Ikegami
Cover Wardrobe	Francis Ocon

First edition, 2001

Manufactured in the United States of America
No lechons were harmed in the making of this book.

Library of Congress Card Number 20010-86843
ISBN 0-9708245-0-5

Contents

vii   Introduction

1   The Making of "the Debut"
by Dawn Bohulano Mabalon

25   Timeline

31   "the Debut"

115   Biographies

123   Credits

Introduction

As we write this introduction, we approach the ninth
anniversary of our work on *the Debut*. We take a moment
to acknowledge the support we have received from you,
our community. With your help, we have been able to
take control of our image in media in order to produce a
multidimensional, positive representation of Filipinos in
America—one of many that we hope will emerge during
this century. We think of the many people who attended
showings, helped pay for our production costs, and
volunteered at film festivals, and who continue to help now
that we are beginning the theatrical release of the film. It is
heartening to see people rallying around the cause of our
community's empowerment through media. With such
support, we are inspired to make sure that the film reaches
its audience by any means necessary. No matter what
happens on the distribution front, the film will be seen.

For those of you who are fans of *the Debut*, we hope this
book will enhance your appreciation of the film and inspire
those who want to tell their own Filipino or Asian
American stories. Within these pages, in addition to the
screenplay you will find a timeline of the film's production,
bios of the cast and crew, and production credits. Dawn
Bohulano Mabalon gives an in-depth account of the
making of *the Debut*, revealing some of the trials and
tribulations of making an independent feature film and
discussing its cultural and historical significance.

You'll notice a number of differences between the published screenplay and the finished film. Our goal is to be as honest and open as possible about the process of writing and producing *the Debut*. Making a film is a constantly evolving process, always vulnerable to a multitude of influences. There is no perfect script. The reality is fraught with mistakes, lines that were changed during shooting, dances cut or reworked, and scenes repositioned. We have included a number of scenes we meant to shoot, but couldn't because of budget and time constraints, and scenes we shot, but deleted because of pacing requirements. We even included scenes that made the final cut, but were produced in ways that were completely different from their original conception in the script.

Despite the difficulties we have undergone in the making of *the Debut*, the process as a whole has given us a larger view of our roles in filmmaking and in the community. It has been a moving and insightful experience. We hope this book will allow you to share that experience with us.

Thank you for supporting our work.

Gene Cajayon
John Manal Castro

The Making of "the Debut"

Dawn Bohulano Mabalon

Since his sophomore year in high school, Gene Cajayon wanted to be a filmmaker. The Saigon-born, U.S.-raised son of a French-Vietnamese mother and a Filipino father, Gene was a self-described "dork" in his Orange County high school. His dream of making films led him to a film degree at Loyola Marymount University, where in 1992 he made a short entitled *Debut* for his thesis. It was about a young Pinoy, his identity crisis, and its eventual resolution at his sister's eighteenth birthday party, or "debut." Almost a decade later, Gene's *the Debut*, one of the first Filipina/o American feature films, premiered to a sold-out crowd in Los Angeles. This essay retraces the film's arduous journey from a student project to a Filipina/o American phenomenon.

In *the Debut*, we meet teenager Ben Mercado, a talented cartoonist whose dreams of Cal Arts may be dashed by his father's insistence on UCLA and medical school. Thoroughly Americanized and alienated from his working-class Filipina/o American family, he is juggling the pressures and tensions of friends, art, school, love, family and identity as his family prepares to celebrate the eighteenth birthday of his sister Rose. At her party, Ben undergoes a transformation as all the disparate elements of his life come together in life-changing experiences with his father, his peers, and an attractive young Pinay.

Gene's vision of a Filipina/o American full-length feature took almost a decade to produce, and the road to its completion in 2000 was not without strife. Major setbacks plagued the production. The script, co-written with filmmaker John Manal Castro, went through almost two dozen re-writes. Hollywood initially embraced the project, only to later dismiss it as not being marketable among mainstream audiences without white actors to star in the leading roles. The film involved some of the brightest Filipino and Filipina/o American talent, but shooting was marred by some extras who threatened to sue when a key Filipino investor bailed during shooting and Gene was broke. It cost almost $1 million to make (huge by indie standards, but tiny compared to Hollywood budgets), and the film put Gene, who partly financed the film using his credit cards, into Chapter 11 bankruptcy. At the completion of the film, an equally drained John was living at home with his parents and slanging video equipment at Fry's Electronics in San Jose. Certainly, the story of *the Debut* is an adventure in Filipina/o American independent filmmaking.

Predictably, the film has been simultaneously embraced and dissed by the notoriously fickle Filipina/o American community. For as many Filipina/os who claim that the film is a reflection of many of their own experiences, there are detractors who have called the film's representations inauthentic and inaccurate. *the Debut* emerges as a host of Filipina/o American filmmakers are producing important, critical work on both coasts and in the Midwest. What sets *the Debut* apart from other work is its sheer scope and budget. While it isn't the first Filipino American feature film (Francisco Aliwalas' 1997 comedy, *Disoriented*, is the first), it is certainly the most hyped, hotly anticipated, expensive, and polished production the community has ever seen. When it finally premiered in the spring and fall of 2000 to audiences in Hawaii, Seattle, San Diego and Los Angeles, it did so with critical acclaim and a warm, if not effusive, reception from Filipina/o American and Asian American communities.

Filipina/o American Film ✪ Coming-of-Age

The first known Filipina/o American film is a silent short by then–University of Southern California film student Doroteo Silva made in the early 1930s. Silva documents the comedy and the tragedy of living as a Filipino in racist Los Angeles. But the catalyst for many of the films made by people of color in the past three decades was a 1967 protest by progressive students and teaching assistants who decried the whiteness and industry-driven nature of the curriculum at the UCLA film school. Film critic Clyde Taylor called it the "L.A. Rebellion" because these film students wanted to make films that served their communities. The rebellion was the beginning of film movements in the Chicana/o, Native American, Pacific Islander, Filipina/o American, and Asian American communities, and of a resurgence of the African American film tradition.[1]

We can trace the emergence of many Filipina/o American filmmakers and their artistic tradition to this movement, and to the influence and visibility of such independent filmmakers of color as Spike Lee and Julie Dash (*Daughters of the Dust*) in the 1980s and 1990s. Institutions that fostered the work of Filipina/o American filmmakers, such as Los Angeles' Visual Communications and San Francisco's National Asian American Telecommunications Association (NAATA), provided support and funding to Pinay and Pinoy filmmakers. As a result, several Filipina/o filmmakers have been producing shorts, documentaries and videos in the past two decades. An incomplete list of Filipina/o American filmmakers includes Matthew Abaya, Mark Arbitrario, Jessica Hagedorn, Rod Pulido (whose film *The Flipside* premiered at the 2001 Sundance Film Festival), Noel Shaw, Angel Shaw, and Celine Parrenas Shimizu.

Many of these filmmakers, including Gene Cajayon and John Manal Castro, are second- and third-generation Filipina/o Americans. *the Debut* emerges as Filipinos are fast becoming the largest Asian group in the United States, and it is important to view *the Debut* in the context of the rapid changes in community history and demographics in the second half of the twentieth century. Though the

Census 2000 numbers have yet to be released, it is projected that Filipina/o American populations will bypass the Chinese population. Already, Filipinos are the third-largest minority group in California after African Americans and Latinos. From the 1920s to the 1960s, Filipina/o American communities were much smaller because of exclusion, anti-miscegenation laws, and a largely male population. When immigration laws changed in 1965 as a response to the Civil Rights movement and economic needs, the demographic change was quick and dramatic—by the 1990s, no other country sent more immigrants to the United States than the Philippines except Mexico. *the Debut*'s central character, Ben Mercado (played by Danté Basco), and his older sister Rose (played by Bernadette Balagtas), are the children of these post-1965 immigrants.

The 1965 Immigration Act encouraged the mass migration of highly trained nurses, doctors, engineers and accountants from all over the world. The abysmal economic and political conditions in the Philippines from the 1960s to the 1980s forced thousands of Filipina/os to search for economic opportunities elsewhere, especially in the United States. Adding to this influx was the recruitment of thousands of men by the U.S. Navy during the 1950s to the 1980s, many of whom brought their families to the United States. The huge Filipino populations in the port cities of San Diego, Vallejo, and Virginia Beach are testament to this. Immigrants based themselves in already established enclaves in Hawaii, and in California cities such as San Francisco, Stockton, San Diego, Seattle, Los Angeles, Carson and Cerritos, West Covina and Chino Hills. Filipino communities mushroomed in such unlikely places as the South, the metropolitan East Coast (New Jersey and New York State), and the Midwest (Chicago).

But if immigration laws opened doors for the new influx of Filipino immigrants, institutional racism would curtail their hopes and dreams. When many highly trained and educated professionals arrived they—like Gina and Roland Mercado, the parents in *the Debut*—found themselves working in low-paid jobs. Filipina/os experienced rampant occupational downgrading. Accountants became cashiers, teachers were forced to be babysitters, surgeons worked as meat-cutters. By the early 1990s, millions of Filipina/o American sons and daughters of these post-1965 immigrants, and grandchildren of pre-1965 immigrants (like myself), were coming of age and approaching their teens, twenties, and thirties, like Ben and Rose Mercado in *the Debut.*

Filipina/o Americans born in the 1970s and early 1980s were raised as the Philippines underwent massive social and political upheaval, and as their parents fled economic disaster in the Philippines to come to an America that promised every opportunity but could deliver little. They were weaned on Schoolhouse Rock, disco, hip hop, punk rock and freestyle, and reached puberty to MTV and the wonders of cable. Those in their twenties and thirties remember too well the cultural racism and right-wing conservatism of the Reagan-Bush era. This generation, the hip hop generation, absorbed all the dynamic and disparate influences around them, as many of them lived in multiracial neighborhoods. Some of Gene and John's influences included the music of Public Enemy, Madonna, The Cure, The Smiths, and Rage Against the Machine, and they watched movies like *The Breakfast Club, Sixteen Candles, Boyz N the Hood*, and *Menace II Society*. In fact, if you watch *the Debut* closely, you might catch the influence of one of Gene and John's favorite (and admittedly, problematic) filmmakers, John Hughes, whose *Sixteen Candles* and *Breakfast Club* were the definitive portraits of angst-ridden '80s white teens.

This generation is the most media-bombarded and technologically savvy of any Filipina/o American cohort. By the 1990s, these largely urban, middle-class and working-class youths were hungry to see themselves reflected in popular culture. Understanding the power of media and weary of constant media invisibility, this generation set out not only to become cultural consumers, but producers as well. The lack of easily identifiable and self-identified Filipina/os in the media frustrated a young John Manal Castro. He recalls, "We were grasping for straws, anyone who was even remotely part-Filipino to claim, like

Phoebe Cates or Prince, to validate our existence." It was a catalyst, he says, to create his own icons, and he turned to role models like Chuck D of Public Enemy, filmmaker Spike Lee and his Make Black Film movement in the '80s and '90s, and Muhammad Ali. John developed a highly politicized aesthetic that critiqued racism and American culture. Many other Filipina/o American artists were doing the similar things in the '80s and '90s.

Perhaps terming the flowering of Filipina/o American artistic and cultural production in the 1990s a "Filipina/o American Cultural Renaissance" pushes the envelope, but the outpouring of Filipina/o American cultural production was very dramatic, and looked very similar to the explosion of Filipina/o American arts that took place in the 1970s.

The 1990s brought the rebirth and creation of Filipina/o American theater groups, film production companies, independent record companies, comedy troupes, film festivals, writer's collectives, Web sites, magazines, 'zines, anthologies, dance companies, arts and culture festivals, designers hawking Filipino-themed T-shirts, publishing companies, and arts collectives. On both coasts, Pinay and Pinoy performance artists, visual artists, poets, comedians, filmmakers, puppeteers, spoken word artists, writers, novelists, dancers, playwrights and musicians produced engaging and cutting-edge work about issues of race, class, gender, sexuality, region, identity and nation. Their work spoke to a multilayered Filipina/o American identity and decried Filipino American arts and media invisibility.

Key to this emergence of a Filipino American arts movement were the exploding populations of Filipino students at state colleges and universities. Though Filipina/o American studies classes were few and far between, those students fortunate enough to take these courses took their lessons to heart. The influence of Filipina/o American studies classes on this generation cannot be overemphasized. Gene and John trace their personal evolutions and *the Debut*'s more political and social themes to the influence of Filipina/o American and Asian American studies courses at Loyola Marymount

University and California State University, Long Beach. Filipino student organizations, particularly Samahang Pilipino at UCLA and Pilipino American Alliance at UC Berkeley, the two longest-running Filipino student organizations, created the now-ubiquitous Pilipino Cultural Nights (PCNs) in which Filipino Americans sang, danced, acted and performed in their own productions.[2] Many artists point to PCNs as their initiation into the world of art and theater.

But little headway in the Filipino American arts could have been made in the 1990s if it weren't for the willingness of Filipino Americans to spend their money on the arts. In a few generations in the United States, Filipina/os learned rapidly that being American has little to do with what you eat or the language you speak, but what you buy. We have become a community of consumption. What drives the Filipino American culture industry is money, and whether earned, borrowed from parents, or scraped together, Filipino Americans have buying power. There was a rapt audience ready to consume the cultural productions and products made by Filipina/o artists in the '90s.

In this past decade, these Filipina/o Americans and their parents spent up to $500 million on Hondas and Acuras, hip hop CDs, Nikes and Adidas, designer clothing, MAC makeup, Polo cologne, and the like. The floors of Southern California's Glendale Galleria and Northern California's mecca, Daly City's Serramonte Shopping Center, have worn thin under the traffic of Filipino American feet. Racer culture has become so ubiquitous in many young Filipina/o American communities that Gene and John comment on it in the film in more than one sequence. In one scene, the film's Filipino cultural nationalist conscience, Edwin (played by Derek Basco), implores his peers to resist the "car conspiracy."

Yet, these same young people have been pouring money (though not in the same numbers, certainly) into the Filipina/o American community. Young Filipina/os have spent thousands on Filipino-themed and -designed T-shirts and clothing, Pilipino Cultural Night tickets, tickets to

Filipino shows and performances, ridiculously expensive debutante balls, entry fees to the circus-like Friendship Games at California State University, Fullerton, and cover charges at dance clubs.

So many dramatic changes were occurring in the Filipina/o American community that in late 1992 as he envisioned his thesis film, *Debut*, Gene could clearly see that his Filipino teen drama about coming-of-age would strike a chord with his community. Gene's experiences mirrored those of many of his peers. He was born in Saigon, Vietnam during the Vietnam War, the son of a Filipino engineer and a French-Vietnamese mother. As an infant, he traveled to Chicago with his parents, where he lived until his parents moved the family to Orange County when he was eight. Like John, Gene felt somewhat of an outsider among his white, Asian, and Filipina/o peers in high school. He was "dissed by all the Asian girls," and had a painful high school experience in Orange County. Growing up with influences from his Filipino and Vietnamese parents, and immersed in American culture, Gene knew early on that he wanted to become a filmmaker. His family didn't think he was serious. "In fact, they still don't think I'm serious," he says.

As a student at Loyola Marymount University, he was deeply influenced by a wide range of American filmmakers, including Ang Lee, whose film, *Eat Drink Man Woman*, was particularly inspiring. He loved Spike Lee ("He is one of the most balls-out, important American filmmakers, and a bad-ass muthafucka"), the cutting-edge director Wayne Wang (*Eat A Bowl of Tea*), and the big, slick, "popcorn movies" like the ones made by James Cameron. He wanted to make the same kinds of entertaining fare—big, slick, Cameron-like movies—with people of color in the main roles. By the time he was finishing his filmmaking degree, Gene had grown frustrated with negative, one-dimensional portrayals of Filipina/os and Asians in the media, and in August 1992, he envisioned a half-hour short film about growing up Filipino in America as his thesis project.

The thesis project became a ten-minute, 16 mm trailer, which he began to use as a fund-raising tool. Throughout

1993, Gene shopped his trailer for *Debut* at several universities and colleges around the country, appealing to Filipino student organizations and their members for support and funding. The feedback he received was instructive, but often brutal. Some Filipina/os connected immediately with the story of Ben, a white-washed Pinoy who comes to terms with his identity at his sister's eighteenth birthday party, but others balked at any attempt to reflect the diversity of contemporary Filipina/o American life "authentically" on film. In San Francisco, Gene's concept came under fierce attack by those who felt he was glorifying the middle-class, privileged culture of affluent Filipina/os by placing a debutante ball (also known as a "cotillion") at the center of his growing-up-in-America story.

The initial short film was a product of Gene's middle-class upbringing. "A lot of the families I knew were doing cotillions," he remembers. "It never occurred to me how fucked up they (debutante balls) were until I was attacked intensely and accused of doing this model minority thing." Gene, a suburban Orange County boy, hadn't given much thought about issues of class privilege surrounding practices like debutante balls. At LMU, he began to take Filipina/o American and Asian American studies classes, which he absorbed "like a sponge," and from them he had an "intense awakening" about Filipina/o American history, culture, and identity. However, he still needed help from somebody who had both working-class consciousness, street credibility, intimacy with the Filipina/o American community, and film expertise. That person was filmmaker John Manal Castro.

When Gene and John hooked up in April 1994, John was still basking in the success of his wickedly funny and satirical 1992 mockumentary on Filipino gangsta culture, *Diary of a Gangsta Sucka*. The film enjoyed critical acclaim, was featured on PBS, and screened at several film festivals. John, a graduate of the film program of California State University, Long Beach, was born and raised in San Jose, California. For John, watching the TV series *Roots* was a pivotal point in his budding political and racial consciousness as a youngster in 1970s East San Jose.

John remembers a "magical" time in the 1980s when his family's garage was a central gathering point for his elder siblings' Filipina/o friends, who "cha-cha'd, rocked, freaked and bus-stopped 'til the break of dawn" to R&B and hip hop as his mother fried lumpia for them.

But like Gene, John grew up feeling like an outsider among his Filipina/o American peers and felt alienated from the high-pressure Filipina/o American youth culture in San Jose, which dictated that all Filipina/os have "the same clothes, cars, hairstyle, and friends" in the 1980s. He turned to underground hip hop and alternative music as an escape because both musics were innovative and broke all boundaries in the '80s. In college, John was influenced by Spike Lee's first films and the writings and speeches of Malcolm X. Furthermore, he was disappointed at the ways Filipina/os were inadequately represented in Asian American Studies texts, and the apathetic ways Filipina/os were representing themselves in popular media ("beauty pageants and Ferdinand Marcos"). After dropping out of Cal State Long Beach because he couldn't figure out what he wanted to do, he enrolled at De Anza Community College, where he had an epiphany. He realized that "film was the only medium powerful enough to put our stories in the spotlight and let the whole world know how dope we were as a people." He went back to Long Beach and enrolled in the film program.

John first heard of Gene's *Debut* project in 1992, when Gene visited Cal State Long Beach's Filipino club to promote his project and raise funds. He didn't see or hear from Gene again until 1994, when he attended another promotional screening for the trailer at Loyola Marymount University. "So the lights dim and the film starts to roll," he recalled in an article written for iJeepney.com. "Immediately I freaked out. The thing is in color and in synch sound! This film had Filipino American actors playing themselves in America!" Inspired, he enrolled in another production class and made *Diary of a Gangsta Sucka*. When it premiered at a small Filipina/o film festival at UCLA in 1994, Gene was in the audience, and they talked. "He told me that he had written a couple of drafts of the feature-length version of *Debut* and wanted me to take a look at it and see what I thought," John recalled. With no post-graduate plans, he thought that working on the script would be "something I could do until I figure things out," he remembers. "It was going to be two weeks of work at the most, I was thinking. Oh, how naïve I was."

Pre-production ✪ 1994–1997

From 1994 to 1995, Gene and John went through an exhaustive process of re-writing. The resulting screenplay was a loosely autobiographical account based on Gene's Orange County upbringing, John's San Jose experiences, and the collective stories of many Filipina/o American friends and relatives. John brought a dose of street credibility and class consciousness to the script. In May 1995, Gene brought the screenplay to Hollywood, and while there was initial interest, no major studio was willing to produce the film. Two of the highest-ranking Filipina/o Americans in Hollywood, Fritz Friedman (an exec at Columbia Tri-Star Home Video) and producer Dean Devlin (*Independence Day* and *The Patriot*), supported the project, and several studios, including 20th Century Fox, Disney, and Columbia Tri-Star, gave the screenplay high praise. But studio executives refused to let Gene have complete artistic control, and they were wary of its all-Filipina/o casting.

According to Gene, studio executives insisted that in order for a film like *the Debut* to become a moneymaker, he would have to cast well-known white actors. "In our case, just finding people in Hollywood that even knew the Filipino American community existed was a challenge," he recalled. "Imagine how difficult it was to get them to even think about financing a film about us. A coming-of-age drama about a Filipino American family? What's a Filipino American?" After a year of shopping the screenplay, Gene decided to go independent.

The film's first significant funding came from a National Asian American Telecommunications Association grant in August 1996. A few months later, Gene paired with

Lisa Onodera, graduate of the UCLA film school, an active partner at Celestial Pictures (an independent film production company based in Santa Monica, California), and an award-winning producer best known for her work on the 1995 film *Picture Bride*. With Lisa's help, *The Mercado Family Debut*, as the film was then known, received the largest public television grant ever awarded to an Asian American feature. Visual Communications signed on as the film's non-profit fiscal sponsor. The filmmakers continued to court individual investors to make up the remainder of the funding needed for the production.

In spring 1997, Lisa and Gene traveled to the Philippines to find additional financing and to find actors to play the adult leads in the film. Quite simply, Gene remembers, they couldn't find actors in the United States to play the adult roles in the play; few first-generation Filipina/o immigrants were actors. They didn't just want good Filipina/o actors; they wanted movie stars. They were rewarded when they cast Filipino superstar Eddie Garcia (Lolo Carlos Mercado), Tirso Cruz III (famous for his roles opposite Nora Aunor), Gina Alajar (Gina Mercado), and beloved Filipino singer and comedienne Fe de Los Reyes (Alice). The actors agreed to work for next to nothing. While in the Philippines, Gene met his future wife, Mabel Orogo. In the course of the making of *the Debut*, they would have two children.

That summer, they cast Danté Basco in the role of Ben Mercado. Danté's charisma made him perfect for the role, Gene recalls. "He was the first person we auditioned…He ripped it up, tore it up. It was amazing to see the words come alive." At that point, Danté was best known for his role as Rufio in Steven Spielberg's *Hook*. Gene had always wanted to cast all of the Basco brothers—actors Derek (Edwin), Dion (Rommel), Darion (Augusto), and Danté—and he was overjoyed when they all agreed to star in the film. It was more difficult to cast Rose Mercado, Ben's sister. Gene was looking for a Pinay who would share a similar phenotype with Danté, as well as have chemistry with him. Actress and comedienne Bernadette Balagtas had the right look and the chemistry they were searching for.

It proved even more difficult to find an actor to play Annabelle Manalo, the best friend of Rose, choreographer of the party's dance scenes, and Ben's love interest. After auditioning dozens of actresses, and only a few weeks before shooting, they found Joy Bisco standing in front of the Palace in Hollywood as a "flier girl" at that club's weekly Legend party, a dance club event that draws hundreds of young Filipina/os from all over Southern California. She had all the elements they wanted—she could act, dance, and convey the right look and attitude. "Annabelle had to be very cool, like a girl from around the way, into hip hop culture, and into the scene," Gene says. The rest of the cast included several first-timers, the singing group Premiere, and Los Angeles fixtures DJ Icy Ice (the founder of Legend Entertainment) and DJ E-man.

Shooting "the Debut" ☉ 1997–1998

When planning for the actual shooting of the movie, Gene felt strongly that the best quality film needed to be made. Though low-budget, the Debut didn't have to look low-budget. "I didn't want to make excuses for a lack of production value," he says. "I wanted to make a movie movie." Additionally, Gene wanted filmmakers of color involved in the production of the film. He hired University of Southern California film school grad Hashim Abed, an Arab-American, as Director of Photography, and recruited as many people of color as possible to round out his crew. "It was like the United Nations," he recalls. "It was very diverse, with Japanese Americans, Latinos, African Americans. It was what Hollywood should be if Hollywood really was the enlightened institution it's supposed to be."

With the film cast and the crew selected, Gene, Lisa, John, and the film's crew spent almost a month of shooting The Mercado Family Debut on location in Southern California beginning in October 1997. Shooting took about twenty-six days total—about twenty-three for principal photography and most of the scenes, and three additional days for re-shooting in 1998. As a first time director, Gene was learning a lot. "I had read about directing in school, but nothing prepares you for the reality," he says. "Nothing prepares you for being on a set the first time." He was concerned with the film's pacing; he wanted the film to be "snappy, poppy, entertaining—first and foremost, a world-class piece of entertainment."

All scenes were shot on location at the school gym of Cantwell Sacred Heart of Mary High School in Montebello, California, and at the house which would serve as the Mercado family's home, located ten minutes away in San Gabriel. Luckily for the money-strapped crew, the principal of the high school they had chosen for the party scenes cut them a break and charged only a percentage of what is usually charged ($2,000 to $3,000 per day) for location use. Gene wanted a nondescript, working-class home for the Mercado family. They had found a house in West Covina, but when that family pulled out at the last minute, they found a house in San Gabriel, only minutes away from the gym. Gene and John felt strongly that the landscape in *the Debut* be "Anytown, U.S.A.," and they refrained from directly identifying the city in the film. However, because Los Angeles is so visually distinctive, they admit that the film still ended up with a very West Coast vibe.

Funding issues haunted the shooting. The project had been rejected by several grant-giving organizations and private investors, so more than $200,000 was charged on credit cards to finance the film. Then, three weeks before shooting began, one key Filipino investor pulled out. He didn't agree to the terms of the investment, and he yanked back his money. "People assumed that we had tons of money because we had lights, trucks, good equipment," Gene recalls. "So they charged extremely high rates." When the movie went broke soon after shooting began, "I spent twelve to fourteen hours a day on the shoot, then at night I got on the phone to hustle and beg for money. Then on the one day I had off, I went to the bank and creatively moved money around to try to find more funding. I begged, borrowed and stole, and maxed out all my credit cards." Gene is quick to point out that none of the film's key staff have ever been paid through the entire eight years of the film's production.

Several major setbacks threatened to stall the completion of the film. During the several years of production, Gene and his wife Mabel had two children, and Lisa also had a child. In fact, there were several babies born to the filmmaking crew; *the Debut* was dubbed "The Fertility Show." In hindsight, he can look back and laugh. "Amazingly enough, we got through it," Gene says. Eventually, he struggled to make payments on the numerous cards he had maxed out paying for the film, and Gene filed for Chapter 11 bankruptcy. In fact, there was so little money that they had to wait until late 1998 to do re-shoots. In the interim, they test-screened a cut of the film to mixed reviews. Test audiences found fault with a variety of scenes and characters, Gene recalls, and they brought extremely high expectations and personal "baggage" to screenings. For example, women hated the character of Annabelle because they felt she was too girly, while men loved her. Gene and John reworked the script for the twenty-first time, cutting fat and adding scenes, and spent three more days re-shooting in November 1998.

Post-Production and Premiere ✪ 1999–2000

In May 1999, the filmmakers changed the film's title from *The Mercado Family Debut* to simply *the Debut*. In September 1999, the film's official Web site, DebutFilm.com, was launched with the creators of pinoynet.com, Eric Ilustrisimo and Ramses Reyes. The response was immediate and overwhelming; more than 150,000 home page hits have registered since its launch. The mailing list boasted 6,000 subscribers, and there were more than 700 postings on the message board. By the year 2000, all editing on the film was completed, and it awaited a final sound mix and titles.

The movie's final touches included assembling a soundtrack that would reflect some of the brightest Filipina/o musical talent. Kormann Roque, who had founded the pioneering

Filipino American-owned and -operated independent record label Classified Records, signed on as Music Supervisor in March 2000. The filmmakers had an open call for Filipina/o American musicians to contribute to the soundtrack of the film, and the respondents included some of the most talented, cutting-edge Filipina/o American artists. The resulting soundtrack features pop, hip hop, R&B and alternative rock, with more than four dozen tracks by Filipino, Filipino American, and Filipina/o Canadian performers, along with a soundtrack by Filipino American composer Wendell Yuponce.

On May 18, 2000, *the Debut* made its World Premiere at the Director's Guild of America Theater as the opening film of the 15th Annual Visual Communications Los Angeles Asian Pacific Film and Video Festival. The film spent the rest of the spring, summer and fall playing to receptive and excited crowds at film festivals in Seattle, San Diego and Hawaii. In March 2001, *the Debut* is the featured selection at the San Francisco Asian International Film Festival, and the weary and elated filmmakers were planning an ambitious self-distribution plan that would bring the movie into every major market.

Political, Cultural and Historic Significance of "the Debut"

The script as written by Gene Cajayon and John Manal Castro, and the eventual movie, attempted to document and comment on many of the issues surrounding young Filipina/o Americans at the turn of the century—identity, class, consumerism, sexual politics, and racism.

First and foremost, Gene and John tackle issues of race and ethnic identity in *the Debut*, and we watch as Ben Mercado eventually realizes that he cannot forsake the Filipino American world he had rejected in favor of the white one he had embraced. "Wake up little brother," Rose tells Ben as he prepares to leave her party with his white friends. "You're just as brown as the rest of us." Ben is stunned when a friend refers to him using a racial epithet, leaving him confused and angry. The film's narrative turns upon this pivotal moment. When Ben realizes that he is as brown as the rest of his friends and family at his sister's party, he returns to the party, where his family, his friends, his girl, and his enlightened future await.

But what being "brown" means in a cultural sense is an important theme for Gene and John. Both felt painfully the exclusion of their peers in high school—both Filipina/o and non-Filipina/o—and they bemoaned the ways that some Filipina/os drew strict boundaries around notions of "authentic" Filipino identity. It was important that Ben's character interrogate essentialized notions of Filipinoness. In other words, it was imperative that Ben would be just as "Filipino" if he were a sensitive artsy type than if he were the archetypical Filipino American male, a macho, gun-toting, gangsta/racer/hip hop head (as in the character of Augusto).

Gene and John were intent to explore these issues of skin color in the film. For example, John says it was important that Annabelle, Rose's best friend and Ben's love interest, be a dark-skinned Pinay. "Growing up watching Filipino films, you never saw dark-skinned Pinays, only light-skinned mestizas," he says. In direct contrast to Philippine cinema's love affair with mestiza/o actors, Gene and John say that they wanted to make a more balanced film that included Filipina/os of varied hues, particularly dark-skinned Filipina/os like Danté Basco and Joy Bisco.

Along with race, gender is a prevalent theme throughout the film. When some Filipina/os heard that the movie was called *the Debut*, they mistakenly believed (myself included) that the central character would be Rose Mercado, the young woman about to turn eighteen and partake in a Filipina/o American rite of passage, the debutante ball, called simply a "debut." According to Gene and John, *the Debut* refers to the individual characters' "debuts" in the film, rather than the birthday party. Instead, Rose's is a secondary story to that of Ben's, the tortured younger son whose own dreams of art school run afoul of those of his father's for him—UCLA and medical school. As both Gene and John readily admit, they're both "guys." They admit in separate interviews that it's difficult to write a female character without her being a love interest. As a feminist Filipina American scholar and artist, it would be easy for me to dismiss the film for its often one-dimensional characterization of Filipinas and Filipina Americans. Rose, Annabelle and mom Gina are the emotional bedrocks for Filipina/o American families, placed squarely in very traditional roles, respectively—the hard-working nanay, the all-knowing ate, and the beautiful Pinay girlfriend.

But that would perhaps be missing the point of the film. While the story may not provide us with multidimensional Pinay characters (though his ate Rose is an endearing character), it does not mean that the movie fails to make statements about gender issues and Filipina/o American sexual politics. It does so from a very male perspective. Closer analysis reveals some interesting statements Gene and John make about struggles over Filipino American maleness and manhood. It is what they know the most about, so it is what they wrote. the Debut is about a Filipino American boy's painful road towards manhood, a journey that requires he make peace with his father, his family, and his ethnic roots and community. Ben's alienation from the macho hypermasculinity of some of his Filipino peers, his white friends, and from his father, uncle and lolo leaves him grappling for a sense of strong Filipino male identity.

Gene and John also felt it important to comment on Filipina/o American sexual politics through the abusive encounter between Augusto and Annabelle, and her romance with Ben. John says he wanted to show how Filipinos and Filipinas can engage in healthy relationships through the relationship of Ben and Annabelle, and that he wanted to create more positive and stronger portrayals of Filipinas. When Ben first encounters Annabelle, she is being verbally abused and physically cornered by Augusto (Dion Basco) at the party; she refuses to give in to him, and Augusto's anger is exacerbated when Ben steps in to intervene. The innocent flirting and attraction between Ben and Annabelle demonstrate Gene and John's concern for, and optimism about, loving and equal relations between Filipinos and Filipinas.

It's also impossible to ignore the issues of class and elitism in the Filipina/o American community as seen through the prism of Rose's "debut" in the film. It was important to Gene and John that class issues play a central role in the film. In *the Debut*, we meet Ben and Rose's father, Roland Mercado, who finds himself in a demoralizing situation. Despite his several years of higher education, he must work as a postman and, therefore, he transfers all his dreams to his son. The Mercados are working-class Filipinos; they live in a modest home in a nondescript, working-class, urban residential neighborhood. It could easily be in Stockton, Carson, or Daly City.[3]

While the film centers mainly around Ben's metamorphosis, *the Debut* is also about Roland Mercado's anxiety regarding his failure to provide his children with the materialist trappings of his class. It's this nagging sense of failure that drives him to ride Ben incessantly to become a doctor. In one solemn scene, Roland apologizes to his daughter Rose for not providing enough for her and the family, and how he feels acutely his working-class status among his more affluent Filipina/o immigrant peers. "These kids today have nicer cars than me," Roland says. "You know Rose, I'm not like your Tito Lenny. Or a lot of the other parents. You gotta go to work, go to school. I can't even afford to buy you a decent car." Rose answers that it doesn't matter to her. "I can't even afford a nice debut for you," he says sadly.

The Mercados are not alone in their inability to pay for an expensive debut. Working-class, even middle-class girls and their families in the Philippines and in the United States might not ever be able to afford the kinds of frothy, over-the-top debutante balls that some Filipino American families beg, borrow and steal to afford. In many traditional debutante balls, an eighteen-year-old Filipina wears a white gown, and is surrounded by attendants who perform a traditional European waltz. An expensive debut is a sure-fire sign of Filipina/o American upper-middle-class status (or, in the case of less affluent Filipina/os, a second mortgage). Rose's eighteenth birthday party is not a "debut" in the conventional sense, for like many Pinays, she is working class. She and Ben are the children of blue-collar parents—their dad is a postal worker, and their mom works in a hospital.

Where more elite Filipino families spend upwards of $10,000 to $15,000 on fancy "hotel debuts" and cotillions at Hiltons and Radissons, Rose has what is more popularly called a "hall party," a party held at the local high school's gym.[4] Debutante balls, Gene says, "promote colonial values and excessive materialism." Instead of scores of waltzing escorts and attendants dressed in Jessica McClintock confections or in similarly ornate home-sewed creations, she and her friends stage an elaborate singkil (choreographed and danced by the Los Angeles–based dance company Kayamanan ng Lahi). If elaborate debutante balls feature expensive hotel chicken and steak dinners, the Mercado guests dine on home-cooked adobo and dinuguan, and a glistening lechon crowns the table.

To the elitist and imperious Lolo Carlos Mercado, who arrives from the Philippines for the affair, his son Roland's failed singing career and his job as a postman are causes for shame. Lolo Mercado smirks in disapproval when he learns that Rose and Ben must work to supplement the family income. Early in the movie, we learn that Tito Lenny, Roland's doctor brother, pays for most of the birthday party. In one dark scene, the patriarch of the Mercado family insults his son by scoffing that the hall party thrown for his granddaughter isn't even a "proper" debutante ball ("maayos na debut"). "So what are you now? A postman! Delivering people's mail!" Lolo Carlos shouts at his son. "You can barely provide for your own family! Can't even afford to give your only daughter a proper debutante ball! If it wasn't for your brother taking care of you, you'd be nothing but a bum on the streets!" Roland and his brother respond angrily, repudiating their father's class values, and we begin to understand the roots of Roland's sense of failed manhood. Gene and John's honesty about the Filipino American working class brought criticism. Said Gene, "One woman approached me after the film and asked, 'Why did you show poor Filipinos? Why not successful Filipinos?'"

Seen in this context and through these issues, the film acts as a sort of fictive ethnography, as it attempts to document and convey so many facets of 1990s Filipina/o American experiences. For that reason, many audiences have taken the film to heart. But moreover, it is an entertaining movie that has also received critical acclaim. It was awarded Best Narrative Feature film at the San Diego Asian American Film Festival in August 2000. In fall 2000, the film won the Audience Award for Best Feature Film at the 20th Annual Hawaii International Film Festival, beating out ninety other films, including Ang Lee's spectacular *Crouching Tiger, Hidden Dragon*. Lines formed around the block for the film's screening at the 2000 Seattle Asian American Film Festival. Emotional e-mails from Filipina/os nationwide praising the film's accuracy at portraying facets of Filipina/o American life continue to bombard the film's Web site, DebutFilm.com. "This movie actually made me feel good about myself," wrote one student in an in-class essay after attending a screening of *the Debut*.

In the film, we see Filipinos as rampant consumers of American and Filipino American culture—we are rampant consumers, obsessed racers stroking our fixed-up Hondas, and working-class youth strutting in overpriced Nikes and North Face puffy jackets. We are hip hop heads, and in the film, we get further validation in our secret beliefs that Filipinos are the dopest dancers and that we have our own style of urban hip hop dance (see the exchange between Pinay and Pinoy dancers at the party). We are young women (Rose and Annabelle) with our family's high expectations and dysfunctions balanced on our shoulders along with friends, school, work, love, and our own dreams.

Filipina/o American parents like Ben and Rose's struggle daily to support their families and tuck away their own failed dreams of upward mobility. We have been and have known those dedicated cultural nationalists who urge their brothers and sisters to resist whiteness and capitalist hedonism (Edwin), for where would we be without them to check us? The movie showcases the vibrancy of Philippine culture as transformed and re-interpreted through Filipino Americans (see the breathtaking singkil performances as done by Kayamanan Ng Lahi). We see the rampant consumerism of Filipina/o American youth as evidenced by their fixed-up Japanese import cars. The violent confrontation between Ben and Augusto highlights the hypermasculinity of much of Filipina/o American youth culture, and the tragedy of Filipino youth violence. Most profoundly, many Filipina/o Americans often experience alienation—from parents, from the outside community, from other Filipina/os, and from non-Filipina/o peers, and can therefore empathize profoundly with Ben's struggles towards self-actualization.

While no piece of cultural work can ever accurately represent the community, the movie is representative of the very community whose cultural priorities and aesthetics created the conditions from which it sprung. If the work of early Pinay and Pinoy filmmakers cracked open the door for Filipina/o Americans to see themselves on the silver screen, the release of *the Debut* tries to kick the door down. The film becomes one more piece of cultural work for Filipina/o Americans to dialogue about and critique, and perhaps its success can inspire more filmmakers, particularly Pinays, to create their own visions and tell their own stories. For as comprehensive as it strives to be, the filmmakers know that *the Debut* only scratches the surface of the Filipina/o American experience. "Rather, the film aims to be merely an opening step in committing our experience in this country to film," says Gene. They hope that the success of the film proves that the Filipina/o American market is a viable one. Certainly, *the Debut* clears the way for many more Filipina/o American filmmakers and their films in the coming years.

NOTES

1   See Toni Cade Bambara's foreword in Julie Dash's book, *Daughters of the Dust: The Making of an African American Woman's Film*, 1992.

2   For a critical analysis of Pilipino Cultural Nights, see Theo
    Gonzalves' article, "'The Show Must Go On': Production Notes
    on the Pilipino Cultural Night," in *Critical Mass: A Journal of
    Asian American Cultural Criticism*, Volume 2, Number 2,
    Spring 1995.

3   Gene and John said they intentionally made the film's location
    regionally unspecific so that Filipino Americans in all areas of
    the country could identify with the landscape as their own
    backyard.

4   Thank you to my colleague and homegirl Dr. Allyson
    Tintiangco-Cubales for introducing me to the term "hall
    party," and for inviting me to all of her own family's famously
    raucous and fun hall parties.

*Dawn Bohulano Mabalon is a third-generation Pinay with
Stockton, California roots. She lives in San Francisco, where
she tells stories as a poet, writer, documentary filmmaker,
performance and spoken word artist, cultural critic, hip hop
scholar and feminist Filipina/o American historian. Her
poetry will appear in the forthcoming Pinay anthology*
Coming Home to a Landscape *(Calyx Books), and her
articles, essays, columns and poetry have been published in*
maganda, Amerasia Journal, Philippine Review, Filipinas,
USA Today/Weekend, *PUSOD's* Call of Nature, *and the*
UCLA Daily Bruin. *She has read poetry and performed in
New York, Seattle, Boston, Houston, Los Angeles, Hawaii, and
throughout the Bay Area. She is a co-producer/director of the
video documentary* Beats, Rhymes and Resistance: Pilipinos
and Hip Hop in Los Angeles *(1999) and is completing her
Ph.D. in American history at Stanford University. Her current
project is a video documentary companion to her dissertation,
entitled "Looking for Little Manila: Filipina/o American
Community in Stockton, California, 1920s–1972."*

Timeline

Conception

February 1992   Fed up with the negative, one-dimensional portrayal of Filipinos and Asians in American media, Writer/Director Gene Cajayon conceives the basic idea and plot for a then-untitled film about growing up Filipino in America. At the time, Gene envisions a half-hour short film that will serve as a thesis project for his film production degree at Loyola Marymount University.

First Draft

August 1992   The first forty-page draft of the screenplay is completed. The working title of the film is now *Debut*. Gene starts to get feedback from readers suggesting that the story might be too large for a half-hour short film.

Trailer

October 1992   Production begins on a ten-minute 16 mm "trailer," which will be used for fund-raising for the full-length version of the project. This trailer also ends up serving as Gene's thesis film for Loyola Marymount University.

Fund-raising

February 1993 The trailer is completed, and Gene starts fund-raising in Filipino and Asian American communities. He decides to go grassroots, showing the trailer to Filipino clubs at universities, Asian business organizations, and Filipino professional groups all across the United States.

John Castro

April 1994 Gene suspends his grassroots fund-raising efforts to concentrate full time on rewriting the script into a full-length feature film with his new writing partner, John Manal Castro.

Hollywood

May 1995 Gene and John complete the 103-page, eighth draft of the script, and Gene shops the screenplay around Hollywood. While response to the writing is strong, no one is interested in actually making the movie because the predominantly Filipino/Asian cast precludes any major white actors from starring in the film.

NAATA

August 1996 After over two dozen rejections from grant-giving agencies, the National Asian American Telecommunications Association (NAATA) awards *Debut* a production grant, the first significant funding the project has secured to date.

Lisa Onodera

October 1996 Gene partners with Lisa Onodera, producer of *Picture Bride*, to raise the remainder of the budget and prepare the film for production.

Pre-production

April 1997 Pre-production begins. Gene and Lisa go to the Philippines to look for additional financing and to cast the adult leads for the film now titled *The Mercado Family Debut*.

Danté Basco

July 1997 Danté Basco is cast in the lead role of Ben Mercado. Tirso Cruz III, Gene Alajar, Eddie Garcia, Fe de Los Reyes, and Ernie Zarate are cast as the adult leads.

Production

October 1997 Five and a half years after Gene conceived the idea of the film, principal photography on *The Mercado Family Debut* begins at Cantwell Sacred Heart of Mary High School in Montebello, California.

Screenings

February 1998 Gene and editor Kenn Kashima complete their first cut of the film. Test screenings begin.

Reshoots

November 1998 Based on the test screening reactions, reshoots begin in Los Angeles. Gene and John are now working on the twenty-first draft of the screenplay.

Music

May 1999 The title of the film is changed to *the Debut* as Gene and Lisa start working on the music licensing for the soundtrack.

pinoynet.com

September 1999   Gene approaches Eric Illustrisimo and Ramses Reynoso of pinoynet.com to develop the Web site for the movie in hopes that it will stir up community support.

Fund-raising

Throughout 2000   Gene and Lisa continue to look for financing to finish the film. The picture is "locked," meaning that all picture editing for *the Debut* is completed, and the film awaits a final sound mix and titles.

World Premiere in Los Angeles

May 2000   *the Debut* has its World Premiere as the Opening Night attraction of the 15th Annual Visual Communications Los Angeles Asian Pacific Film and Video Festival. Demand is so high that tickets to the event sell out in less than a day, and an overflow theater is opened to accommodate the entire crowd. Later, the encore screening is packed with supporters from all over the U.S.

San Diego Asian Film Festival

July 2000   Hailed as "a film that is groundbreaking to the community it serves," *the Debut* wins Best Narrative Feature Film at the San Diego Asian Film Festival. The attendance is outstanding as the Opening Night screening of *the Debut* sells out after the publicity generated from the Los Angeles world premiere.

Seattle Asian American Film Festival

October 2000   *the Debut* closes out the 2000 Seattle Asian American Film Festival. The Filipino American community in Seattle packs the exclusive one-time screening. Film supporters, anxious to purchase their tickets in advance, form a line outside the Seattle Cinerama hours before the box office opens.

UCLA Showcase

October 2000   *the Debut* cast members host the UCLA Showcase, an annual staple promoting Filipino and Asian American music. The audience is also treated to a screening of the trailer and a music video featuring R&B group Pinay.

Hawaii International Film Festival

November 2000   The film takes home the festival's coveted Audience Award for Best Feature Film. Awards Night host and critic Roger Ebert endorses *the Debut* with a "Hang Loose/Thumbs Up." Positive word-of-mouth from early screenings brings bigger audiences to two subsequent ones. Much of the film's success in Hawaii is the result of a grassroots promotional campaign orchestrated by the crew and volunteers. Promotional events include talks at the University of Hawai'i and an appearance on radio station KNDI 1270-AM.

San Francisco International Asian American Film Festival and San Francisco Release

March 2001   *the Debut* has its theatrical release on Closing Night of the San Francisco International Asian American Film Festival. Soon after, it will spread to theaters throughout the San Francisco Bay Area. Following this, it will tour the U.S. and Canada. Theatrical release in the Philippines is planned for December 2001.

the Debut

Gene Cajayon and John Manal Castro

5 Card Productions
Santa Monica, California

Revised January 6, 2001

Note

Since there was never a true final draft of the script, we put this one together based on several different versions of the shooting and reshoot drafts. You'll notice there are scenes that we shot, but that didn't make the final cut as well as scenes that we think are cool, but that we couldn't shoot due to budget constraints. All in all, we think it's a faithful representation of the final film with some nice extras thrown in for true fans of the movie.

Gene Cajayon
John Manal Castro

Fade in.

Close up on a blank sketch pad. As the main titles start to roll, a hand holding a pencil moves into frame and starts drawing. An easygoing alternative rock groove starts kicking on the soundtrack.

Extreme close up of an eye—almond-shaped, dark brown, Malaysian descent, concentrating hard on the sketch pad.

Extreme close up of a Polaroid photo of several white high school students. Attractive, well-groomed, dressed well in expensive clothing.

Back to the pad. The artist completes a skillful thumbnail sketch of the students.

Extreme close up of the artist's lips biting the pencil.

Close up on a new Polaroid. More white high school students, this time hanging out around a late-model BMW.

Back to the pad. Another skillful sketch. The artist is obviously talented.

So goes the rhythm of the title sequence—dissolving and cutting back and forth between extreme close ups of our mysterious artist, his sketches, and his Polaroids, cut to the beat of the music.

Most of the candid Polaroids are at a high school. All the subjects are white, and all seem to be part of the same tight clique. The artist's drawings are passionate, filled with empathy for his subjects.

We end the title sequence by slowly zooming out to a wider shot of the sketch pad, now covered with drawings. The Polaroids are littered about the outer edge of the pad, forming a frame around the collage of sketches.

Fade to black.

Fade in.

Int. Comic book store – day

We are looking at a glass counter top, underneath which are pasted various colorful comic book art. Two long, rectangular boxes filled with comic books suddenly plop down over it. We pan over to Ruben ("Ben"). He takes a deep breath.

Ben   That's the last of them.

The store is densely decorated and stocked with every possible genre of comics as well as hundreds of other collectible cards, action figures, magazines and toys. Next to Ben behind the counter is Doug (17, Caucasian) and his cheery ex-hippie dad, Dave (40s). Doug starts sifting through one of the boxes.

Doug   Damn, that's a lot of books.

Dave   You sure you want to do this, Ben? I mean, I feel really guilty here.

Ben nods, apprehensive, looking at the stacks of books.

Ben   Yeah. I'll get 'em back someday.

Doug pulls several comics out of the boxes as Dave pulls out a thick, black business check binder.

Doug   Damn. Look at that, the first Gambit. Oh shit, Hulk 181! X-Men 94! This is some collection you got, Ben.

Dave   Biggest one I've ever bought.

A customer steps up to the counter with several comic books. Ben takes them and starts ringing them up.

Ben   Well, you sold most of them to me. *(to the customer)* $3.42, please.

Dave   *(chuckling)* Yeah, I guess you're right. So this is it for you, huh?

Ben   Yeah. Puts me over the top. *(counting out the change)* Four and five. Thanks.

The customer leaves as Dave hands Ben the check.

Dave   Here you go, kiddo.

Ben takes the check and stares at it. Doug looks over his shoulder.

Doug   Fuck. I could buy a nice car for that, Pop.

Dave	It's called a savings account, Doug.

Ben laughs as he and Doug head for the exit.

Ben	Thanks again, Dave.
Dave	Just don't forget us when you're rich and famous.
Doug	See you tonight, Pop.
Dave	Hey, Ben. *(Ben stops, turns)* Congratulations.

Ben cracks a wide grin as they exit and we

Ext. Van Go's Ear parking lot – day, afternoon

Doug and Ben walk up to a '67 midnight blue Ford Mustang, which is parked head out in a handicapped parking space in front of a coffee house. Like the cast from a Fox teen drama, numerous white high school students are hanging out all around the scene.

Like the token black guy in an Aaron Spelling TV show, Ben stands out as the only person of color in a sea of Waspiness. He gingerly holds the check in his hand.

Doug	You know how much damage you can do with that?
Ben	Yeah, six-grand worth.

Doug slaps the hood of the Mustang.

Doug	Ben, Vegas! Rick'll drive! All of it on black, let's go!

Ben laughs as Christian (17) walks past the guys and slaps Ben on the back.

Ben	Hey, whussup, man.
Doug	Hey, Chris.

Ben turns and smiles at Jennifer Conrad (17), a sweet blonde walking by with Susie (18) and several cute white girls (16–18). All are carrying lattes and mochas.

Jennifer glides over.

Susie	Jennifer, come on, we gotta go.

Jennifer	Yeah, just a sec.

Susie and the other girls head for Susie's new Toyota 4-Runner parked next to the Mustang.

Jennifer	Hi, Ben.
Ben	Hey, Jennifer. Hey, what's that?

Ben notices a portfolio under her arm and cocks his head to the side for a better view.

Say…that's pretty good.

She half-turns away and starts to blush.

Jennifer	Huh? No, it's nothing. Just my final project.
Ben	Harper's class? C'mon, lemme see.

She reticently places it in his hand. He checks it out.

Hey, this is beautiful.

Jennifer sidles up next to Ben. Their arms just barely touch as she reaches out to support the portfolio.

Jennifer	Stop. Really?

Jennifer turns to Ben. Stray hair brushes against his cheek. Their faces are inches away.

Ben	Yeah. Your use of light…the shadowing. It's good.

Susie sticks her head out the window of her 4-Runner.

Susie	Jennifer!

Jennifer turns and shouts gruffly.

Jennifer	Hang on!
Susie	*(to her passengers)* What is up with her?
Jennifer	I gotta go.
Ben	I can tell.

Ben hands her the portfolio.

Jennifer	See you at Sheldon's party. You're going, right?
Ben	Yeah, of course.

Doug steps up and tries to look cool as they watch Jennifer getting into Susie's car.

Doug   Dude, she's on your nuts like a squirrel.

Ben   (*suddenly remembering*) Ah, damn. When's Sheldon's party?

Doug   Tomorrow. Why?

Susie shoots an annoyed look at Ben as she pulls away.

Ben   My sister's birthday party is tomorrow night.

Doug   Uh, help me out here, Ben. Cake and ice cream, or ten kegs and Jennifer Conrad in a miniskirt.

Ben   Shit.

Doug   You're going to Sheldon's. End of story.

Ben   Doug, they've been planning this thing for a long time. My uncle shelled out much money, I got relatives flying in… What do you want me to do? Just skip it?

Doug simply stares at Ben.

Doug   Yeah. Why not?

Ben laughs good-naturedly as Doug pulls out a tacklebox-style art supply bin and plops it on the trunk of the Mustang.

Ben   What's that for?

Doug   For you, what do you think?

Ben   Ah, for real.

Doug   Just a little something to mark the occasion. You like it?

Ben   This is too cool, Doug. I really need one of these.

Ben picks it up. It's heavy.

Doug   Go on, open it.

Ben opens it and pulls out several bottles of beer on ice.

Doug   That was Rick's idea.

Ben laughs as we

Ext. Ben's neighborhood – day, late afternoon

Series of shots. Rick's Mustang cruises through a working-class, industrial neighborhood.

Ext. Mercado home – day, late afternoon

Establishing. The Mercado house is a modest, working-class residence in an older, blue-collar neighborhood. Single-story bungalows, cars parked on lawns, weeds peeking through cracks on the sidewalks, graffiti.

Stereo blaring alternative rock music, Rick's Mustang pulls up to Ben's house. Ben gets out and taps the car's hood.

Ben	Thanks for the ride, guys.

Ben quickly heads for the front door. Doug and Rick (18) get out, follow Ben.

Doug	Ben, wait up. I gotta pour my tea.
Ben	Why didn't you go at the mall?
Doug	'Cause I didn't have to go then.
Ben	Can't you wait?
Doug	Dude, I'm gonna explode, man.

Ben just stares at his buddies, hesitating opening the front door.

Doug & Rick	What?
Ben	All right, come on, just hurry up.

Ben opens the door and they go inside.

Int. Mercado living room – day, continuous

We can now hear sounds of food cooking, loud talking and laughing from down the hallway.

Ben, Doug and Rick enter.

Doug	What's going on, Ben? Sounds like a party.

Embarrassed, Ben hastily escorts Doug to the bathroom.

Ben Don't you have something to do?

Rick Damn, dude, what's that smell?

Ben I'll be back in a second.

Ben heads for the kitchen.

Rick Making me hungry again.

Int. Kitchen – day, continuous

A madhouse. Ben's mother Gina, Tita Connie and Tita Florie (Aunties, 40s) are busily preparing a huge amount of food. Tito Lenny (50s) is at the counter writing out checks. Ben's ebullient uncle, well-dressed in a designer suit, breaks into a wide grin as Ben enters.

Tito Lenny Hoy, the next doctor of the Mercado family!

Gina Where have you been, Ruben?

Ben Hi, Tito Lenny. Can you turn on the fan, Mom? The house smells.

Ben starts struggling to open the windows in the kitchen. Tito Lenny puts his arm around his nephew.

Tito Lenny You'll have some drinks with your uncle tomorrow, ha? Grow some hair on your chest.

Ben Hairy chest? Can't turn that down.

Int. Living room – day, continuous

Rick is checking out the typical middle-class Filipino American decor—seashell lamps hanging from the ceiling, an altar to Jesus and the Virgin Mary, an organ gathering dust. On top of the organ is a small wooden statue of a naked man wearing a removable barrel.

Rick lifts up the barrel and is pleasantly surprised when a giant, spring-loaded wooden penis pops up.

Doug comes out of the bathroom, finds Rick messing around with the barrel man.

Rick   Doug, check this out. *(lifts up the barrel)* That wicked or what?

Int. Kitchen – day, continuous

Dressed in his postal uniform, Ben's father Roland (40s) enters from the backyard, where we can hear loud chatter from a group of teenagers. Ben is still struggling with the window.

Roland   Hoy, do you know what time it is? *(no response from Ben)* Hanging out with your friends again, wasting your time.

Roland takes a tray of drinks off the counter.

You get cleaned up and help your mother, ha?

Ben   Yeah, whatever.

A tense, silent beat as Roland heads back out and Ben finally forces open the window. Tito Lenny tries to lighten the mood.

Tito Lenny   I know you're not a doctor yet, Ben, but I have a condition you might be able to diagnose.

Ben   What's that?

Tito Lenny   Well, every time I see your Tita Connie in her nightgown, I get this swollen feeling in my lower abdominal area.

The whole kitchen starts laughing as Tita Connie slaps Tito Lenny on the shoulder.

Tita Connie   Bastos, Lenny! Why do you talk like that in front of Ben?

Tito Lenny   Oh, it's okay. My nephew is a grown man already, ha Ben? Tell your auntie you're a grown man.

Ben   I'm a grown man.

Tito Lenny   You see? No worries. *(to Ben)* When you need recommendations for med school, remember to ask me, ha?

Ben   Uh, sure.

Suddenly, everyone falls silent and turns to the hallway as if a monster has appeared.

Doug & Rick	*(waving)* Hi there!
Gina	Who is this?

Gina starts walking up to Doug and Rick. Ben runs past her and takes them both by the arm.

Ben	Friends from school. They just had to use the bathroom. Let's go, guys.
Gina	What are your names? I've never seen you before.
Ben	This is Doug, and this is Rick. Guys…

Ben nudges his friends to move along.

Gina	So you go to school with Ben?
Rick	Yeah, we're really good friends.
Gina	You should come by more often. We never get to see Ben's friends.
Doug	Ben never invites us, that's why.
Gina	Are you guys hungry? We have plenty to eat.
Rick	Um, yeah…

Doug notices the huge, three-foot-long wooden fork and spoon hanging on the wall. Points it out to Rick.

Doug	You must get big portions here.
Ben	They already ate, Mom. Come on, guys.

Ben corrals the guys like cows and pushes them to the

Int. Hallway – day, continuous

Ben briskly walks them to the door.

Rick	Dude, what's the big rush?
Doug	We don't have to go.
Ben	Yes, you do.
Gina (o.s.)	Hoy! Don't be rude! Let me give them something to take home!
Doug	We have time for a bite.

Ben	What, your parents don't feed you?

Ben practically shoves them out the front door.

Rick	Hey, Ben, where can I get one of those naked barrel dudes with the monster-size…

Ben	Try Wal-Mart. Bye.

Hold on an obviously embarrassed Ben as he shuts the door behind them. Time cut to

Ext. Backyard – night, later

A raucous group of seventeen Filipino teenagers (14–19) is rehearsing traditional Filipino dances on the lawn. Annabelle (19), a pretty Filipina in baggy jeans and a Pinay T-shirt, is giving instructions.

Annabelle	Remember guys, four counts and then turn.

To their side are Titos Dante and Boy (40s) playing a guitar and a mandolin, respectively. Roland comes up and takes away the now-empty tray of drinks.

Tito Dante	Hoy, Roland, why don't you join in? Sige na! For old time's sake!

Roland snorts, amused, then heads back inside the house.

Int. Hallway – night

Roland is about to step into the bathroom when he notices Ben's bedroom door is closed and the lights are on inside.

Int. Ben's bedroom – night, continuous

Ben is at his drafting table, writing intently in a California Institute for the Arts course catalog. Suddenly, Roland barges into the room. Ben shoves the catalog under a bunch of sketches and pretends he's drawing.

Roland	Ruben! What are you doing?

Ben	Don't you know how to knock?

Roland	What?
Ben	(*still not turning around*) Pop, do you mind? I'm trying to get some work done.

Roland stomps up to Ben, sees what Ben is drawing.

Roland	What is this? What are you doing?
Ben	Homework. What does it look like?
Roland	You lazy child! I told you half an hour ago to go help your mother with the food!

Ext. Backyard – night, continuous

The dancers and band members are listening in on the argument, plainly audible through Ben's window. Rose shakes her head, embarrassed.

Ben (o.s.)	I'll be there in a minute, Pop.

Int. Ben's bedroom – night, continuous

Roland	You know we have been working so hard for your sister's party, and you still go gallibanting around.
Ben	(*correcting his accent*) I wasn't gallivanting. I was working.
Roland	And then you come home and don't dare lift a finger to help! (*Ben starts drawing again*) Get up!
Ben	I said I'll be there soon.

Roland slaps the back of Ben's head. Ben finally turns, glaring defiantly at his dad.

Roland	Goddammit! Are you listening to me? Stop with those stupid pictures!

Ben turns back around.

Ben	(*under his breath*) Fuck this shit.
Roland	What did you say?!

Roland grabs Ben's pencil and makes a big mark across the sketch.

Ben   Hey!

Roland and Ben are now both holding the pencil, both trying to pull it away. A tug-of-war ensues. Roland starts cursing loudly in Tagalog.

What are you doing?!

Realizing how silly they must look, Ben lets go. Roland is pulling so hard, he stumbles back several steps and runs into Gina, who is now standing in the doorway. Gina props Roland up and he regains his balance.

Gina   Tama na! Everybody can hear you!

Ben stares at his dad like he's a psychotic.

Roland   Goddamn disrespectful child!

Roland storms out of the room. A long, tense beat.

Gina   Every time like this.

Gina leaves. Ben stares at the ruined sketch, fuming. Time cut to

Int. Rose's bedroom – day, morning

Feminine decor, practical and efficiently organized. Rose is sound asleep. Outside her window we hear the sounds of someone playing basketball.

Bam! A basketball hits the window pane.

Rose awakens with a start. She goes over to the window and peeks through the blinds. Time cut to

Ext. City street/Mercado driveway – day

Rack focus from the Vincent Thomas Bridge in the background to a basketball hoop in the foreground. A basketball banks off the backboard and bounces into the net as we

Ext. Mercado driveway – day, moments later

Ben is at three-point range, shooting at the basketball net mounted above the garage. The front door opens and out steps Rose. Quiet tension as she just stands there watching Ben. After a long beat…

Ben   Morning to you, too.

Rose   Enjoyed the show last night.

Ben snorts, then shoots a basket. Makes it.

Couldn't you have chilled for just one night?

Ben   Why don't you tell him that.

Rose   Listen, Ben, I know you think all this is stupid, but you could have avoided the whole thing with Pop just by helping out a little.

Ben doesn't answer and shoots another basket.

If it makes you happy, why don't you just not go today.

Ben   Maybe I won't. All I'm gonna see anyway is a bunch of punks giving me attitude. And aunties with orange hair bugging me to see if I have a girlfriend or not. I don't need that shit.

Rose just stares at Ben, incredulous.

Rose   Whatever.

Rose heads back inside. A moment passes. Then Rose comes marching back out.

You know, I cannot wait for you to leave for UCLA 'cause I am sick of dealing with your stupid shit.

Ben   UCLA? Try Cal Arts.

Rose   What?

Ben   I'm going to Cal Arts.

Rose   Very funny, Ben.

Ben shoots another basket.

Ben   I'm serious. I went over there last Friday and paid off my first year's tuition.

Rose   You don't have that kind of money.

Ben   I don't now. I dumped all my savings. I even sold most of
        my comics.

Rose   You did it?

Ben   I'm penniless, but I'm enrolled.

Rose   Pop's gonna shit.

Ben   Fuck him.

Rose   *(walking up to Ben)* How many times do we have to go
        through this? You gotta tell him your real plans. Especially now.

Ben   Easy for you to say. He worships you. All he's gonna say is…
        (mimicking Roland's accent) "What kind ub job are you
        going to get drawing cartoons?"

        *Rose grabs Ben's face with both hands and forces him to face
        her.*

Rose   But Ben, you're in! The first year's paid for. Just talk to him.

        Ben grabs her face with both hands too, mimicking her.

Ben   Listen, Rose, I don't need his help or his approval. So drop it.

        *They stand in the driveway, looking silly as they hold each
        other's heads in their hands.*

Rose   I've warned you way too many times. You're on your own,
        little brother.

Ben   Right. So quit lecturing or I'm going to have to learn you
        something.

        Attitude flowing, Ben tosses her the ball.

Rose   'Cause of course, Cal Arts guy knows everything.

Ben   That's right.

        *She starts dribbling the ball and droppin' 'tude right back
        at him.*

Rose   To five?

Ben   Maybe you can sweat some pounds off so you can fit in
        that dress of yours.

Rose   Don't worry, Ben, I'll be gentle.

Ben   You're not wearing any shoes.

Rose   Your handicap. You know, like golf?

Int. Roland & Gina's bedroom – day, continuous

Roland is in front of a mirror, hands shaking, trying to knot his tie. Next to him is Gina getting into a pretty, full-length dress.

Roland   Hay, nako.

Gina   H'wag kang mag-alala, Roland. Nakahanda na ang lahat. It's going to be okay.
[Don't worry anymore, Roland. Everything's ready. It's going to be okay.]

Roland   Kumusta na ba siya?
[How is he anyway?]

Gina   Sabi ni Lenny may jet lag pa. A las kuwatro ng madaling araw na dumating.
[Lenny said he's jet-lagging badly. His flight came in at four this morning.]

Roland yanks down hard on his tie, frustrated.

Here, let me do that.

(Starts knotting Roland's tie) Relax ka lang. Siguro tutuksuhin ka lang naman tungkol sa…
[Relax. He'll probably just make fun of your…]

Gina pokes Roland's stomach. He frowns at her.

Gina   Just kidding! Susmaryosep, sobra ka namang seryoso. Sigurado ako na matutuwa siya kapag nakita niya si Rose at si Ben. Tiyak na makakalimutan niya ang lahat.
[Just kidding! God, you're too serious. I'm sure he'll be so thrilled just to see Rose and Ben that he'll forget everything.]

Roland   Ay, Gina, kilala mo naman siya.
[Oh, Gina, you know how he is.]

Gina   Well, you'll only make it worse if you keep worrying.

Gina finishes Roland's tie. They turn to the mirror.

Ayan. You look good.

Roland   *(frowning)* I look old.

Gina   You're not old. If you're old, then I'm old. And I'm not old.

Gina goes to a stereo sitting on the dresser and turns it on. A Tagalog love song starts playing as she walks back up to Roland and holds her arms up. He smiles, nerves melting away, and takes her into his arms.

They start to waltz. Both move very gracefully. Beautifully. Dancing cheek to cheek, Roland starts quietly singing the song to Gina as she places her head on his shoulder.

Ext. Driveway – day, continuous

A downhome, lip smackin', finger lickin', infectious bass groove kicks in as we start a montage of high energy b-ball playing.

Ben and Rose are both very good. Rose works some amazing moves in her bare feet. Ben's not shy about playing rough, and neither is Rose.

The game builds to a 4–4 tie when suddenly Titas Connie and Florie come out of the house. They snap their fingers at Ben and Rose as they head for Tita Florie's minivan parked in the street.

Tita Florie   Hoy! What are you two doing out here?

Tita Connie   You're going to be late!

Rose   Oh sorry, Tita.

Rose is distracted, and Ben makes a shot over her. He throws his hands up in the air triumphantly.

Ben   Game! Thank you very much!

Ben starts inside, gloating. Pouting, Rose follows.

Rose   No fair, I wasn't paying attention.

Ben   Tough shit. I do believe you owe me the car next weekend.

She grabs the ball.

Rose	So are you down for my party or what?

Ben heads inside.

Ben	Yeah, all right.
Tita Connie	Come inside now, you're going to get too dark.

The bass groove fades out and a Tagalog party song fades up as we make a time cut to

Int. Hallway – day, later

Ben cruises into his bathroom to take a shower. Down the hall Roland walks out of another bathroom, half-dressed in a suit. Their eyes meet for a moment, then quickly both look away and head their separate ways.

Int. Rose's bedroom – day, continuous

Dressed in an elegant, white cocktail dress, Rose is getting her hair worked on by Gina.

Ext. Driveway – day, continuous

The Titos and Titas are loading Tita Florie's minivan with trays of food.

Int. Living room – day, later

Close on a row of framed family photos on the mantel above the fireplace. Pan over to the center of the room where Gina and Rose are posing for a picture. Flash! Then Rose, Gina and Roland. Flash! Rose and a very bored Ben. Rose elbows him in the side, telling him to smile.

Several people with cameras are working at one time—a professional photographer (40s), his partner, a videographer (20s), and Tita Connie with her trusty Polaroid.

Flash! White out to

Ext. Catholic parish – day, afternoon

Establishing—Tita Florie's minivan, the Mercado family van conversion and Tito Lenny's Cadillac drive into the parking lot of an old, gothic Roman Catholic church. The caravan pulls up to the gymnasium behind the church, next to the rectory and grade school.

Int. Gymnasium – day, continuous

Establishing. Decked out in bright, festive decor. A large dance area in the center is surrounded by numerous dinner tables. At the front are the buffet tables and a raised stage area.

Int. Buffet tables – day, continuous

Gina and the Titas are unwrapping the food and setting it up over warmers. Loving, mouthwatering close-ups of the dishes they worked so hard to prepare.

Tito Lenny tries furtively to take some food to munch on, but Tita Connie shoos him away.

Int. Stage – day, continuous

Two Filipino disc jockeys, DJ Icy Ice (25) and DJ E-man (25), and three Filipino assistants (18–21) are setting up an elaborate turntable, lighting and speaker system.

Int. Gymnasium – continuous

Series of quick-cut shots as various family members put the last streamers, place settings, balloons, and other decorations into place.

Int. Buffet tables – day, continuous

Two Filipino delivery men place a metal platter holding a huge roast pig (lechon) on the buffet table.

Close on the Titas and Titos all gathered around the lechon and smiling excitedly.

Tita Florie Now it's a party.

Time cut to

Int. Gym main entrance – night

The Mercado family and Father Bob (60s, white, Roman Catholic priest) are lined up, greeting in turn the dozens of guests lining up at the main entrance. Ben and Rose are at the head, followed by Gina, Roland and Father Bob. The photographer and videographer move up and down the line, documenting.

Next in line is Alice Johnson (40s), a boisterous Filipina in a loud red dress with orange-tinted hair, carrying a huge, brightly wrapped present. Followed by her disaffected husband, George Johnson (white, 50s).

Alice Hi, Rosemary! Happy happy birthday! You look so beautiful! Oh, you remember my husband George.

George Hello, happy birthday. Mabuhay.

Elated, she turns to Ben and grabs his cheek.

Alice Who is this?

Gina Ay, Alice, you remember Ben? My youngest.

Alice dishes off the present to George, takes Ben's arm.

Alice Oh, he's so handsome now! Guwapo-guwapo naman! You have a girlfriend already, ha?

Ben Uh, no.

Alice How come you didn't come to my wedding last year?

Ben Sorry, had to work.

Alice Well, aren't you going to give me a kiss?

Grimacing, Ben gives Alice a kiss on the cheek.

Ay, Ben! You remember my son, your old friend Augusto!

Alice and George step to the side, revealing Augusto, who is followed closely by Nestor and Rommel (17–19, Filipino American). All three are doing the Filipino Roughneck Gangsta bit—shaved heads, oversized T-shirts, baggies, attitude the size of an island nation.

(to Gina) Augusto brought his friends. I hope you don't mind.

Alice grabs Augusto and pushes him to Ben.

Here! Say "hello" to your old playmate!

Augusto looks highly embarrassed in front of his crew. Ben tries to hide his look of sheer disgust.

Augusto	Mom…

Alice slaps Augusto on the head. Nestor and Rommel snicker.

Alice	Hoy! Say "hi" you rude boy!

Ben and Augusto's eyes lock briefly, then turn away.

Augusto	Ben…
Ben	'Sup.
Alice	(to Gina) Hay! These kids, so strange!

Int. Buffet tables – night, continuous

Tita Connie and Tita Florie observe Alice's family as they leave the greeting line.

Tita Connie	Hoy! Connie! Tingnan mo naman si Alice. Akala mo kung sino…porke nakahuli siya ng puti. [Hey, Connie! Look at that Alice. She thinks she's so great. Just because she hooked a white guy.]
Tita Florie	Well, I heard from Gina that he's impotent.
Tita Connie	Impotent?
Tita Florie	You know—his birdy cannot fly.

The Titas start giggling hysterically.

Int. Gym main entrance – night, continuous

Led by Tito Lenny and his sons Edwin (21) and Jun (18), Lolo Carlos (70s) makes his grand entrance. Gina grabs Ben, whispers in his ear.

Gina Oh oh! Ben! Your grandfather!

Tito Lenny Kids, your Lolo Carlos.

Lolo Carlos smiles as he takes Ben and Rose by the arms.

Lolo Carlos Hello, hello! My goodness, look at you two kids! Ang lalaki na pala ng mga apo ko!
[My grandchildren are so big already!]

Rose takes his hand and places it on her forehead.

Rose *(practiced)* Mano po, Lolo. Maraming salamat ho at nakarating po kayo dito para sa birthday ko.
[Bless, Lolo. Thank you so much for coming to my birthday here.]

Lolo Carlos Oh! Ang galing mo pala managalog, Rosemary. *(takes her head in his hands)* Napakaganda…kamukha mo ang iyong Lola, anak.
[You speak very good Tagalog, Rosemary. So beautiful… you look like your grandmother, child.]

Rose Maraming salamat po, Lolo.
[Thank you very much, grandfather.]

Lolo Carlos turns to Ben, takes him by the arms.

Lolo Carlos At si Ruben, ha? Sino 'tong higanteng 'to?
[And what about Ruben? Who is this giant here?]

Not understanding Tagalog, Ben looks intimidated.

Lolo Carlos Handsome boy, 'no?

Lolo Carlos holds his hand out to Ben for his mano (blessing). Instead, Ben shakes it. Carlos gives him a curious look, then laughs.

Aba…binata na pala 'to. Hindi na nagmamano sa kanyang matandang Lolo, 'no?
[Well…this one's grown up already. Too grown up to ask his grandfather's blessing, right?]

Polite chuckles as Lolo Carlos pats Ben's shoulder good-naturedly. He then takes both Rose and Ben by the arms, eyes sparkling.

So beautiful together, ha? The last time I saw the two of you, you were both babies. Now look at you two.

Lolo Carlos stands there, staring at his grandchildren for a long, awkward moment.

Tito Lenny   Oo, Pa. Si Gina.

Lolo Carlos finally moves down the line to Gina.

Lolo Carlos   Kamusta, iha?
[How are you, my dear?]

Gina   Mabuti naman, Papa. Tuwang-tuwa kami na nandito ho kayo.
[Fine, Papa. We're so happy that you are here.]

Lolo Carlos smiles stiffly. He turns to Roland, who is shifting nervously, sweat collecting on his brow.

Roland   Hello, Pa.

Lolo Carlos looks Roland up and down for a long, tense moment, assessing his younger son.

Lolo Carlos   Roland. Tamaba ka yata.
[Looks like you've gained some weight.]

Roland and everyone around him laughs nervously.

Tito Lenny   Pa, let's go sit down, ha?

Tito Lenny leads Lolo Carlos away to the dinner tables.

Angle on Roland as he relaxes, exhaling deeply. Gina places a comforting hand on her husband's shoulder. Time cut to

Int. Buffet tables – night, later

Guests are lined up, helping themselves to food. The Titas are behind the tables, proud their work is finally being enjoyed. The photographer and videographer again are covering the line.

Int. Vasquez/Johnson table – night, continuous

George, Alice, Augusto, Nestor and Rommel are eating with Tita Florie and Tito Dante.

Tito Dante   When Florie first started at the hospital, there were hardly any. Now almost half the hospital's nursing staff is Oriental.

George   You really should say Asian. Oriental is a very touchy word today. The proper term to use now is Asian when referring to people from the Far East.

Alice   *(cutting George's steak)* I didn't know that. How interesting.

George   Not so small, honey.

Tita Florie   Anyway, now we have Orientals, Filipinos, Mexicans, Blacks…

George   It's funny though, because Filipinos are not really considered part of the Asian race. They're part of the Malay race.

Alice   You're so smart, honey. *(to Dante and Florie)* That's why I love him.

Smirking, Rommel nudges Augusto, who looks like he's about to beat up George.

Int. Mercado table – night, continuous

Flash! Tita Connie takes a Polaroid of Gina and Rose at the table.

Tita Connie   Ayan. Thank you.

Ben sits with his family, Lolo Carlos, Father Bob and Tito Lenny's family. He is distant, looking around the gym.

Hoy, Roland, Ben. Let me get a picture of you with Lolo Carlos. *(no one moves)* Come on, let's go!

The three generations stand up and tentatively move together.

Okay…closer…now smile…

Rose   Come on, you guys look like statues. Smile!

Flash! Ben doesn't waste any time getting back to his seat.

Tita Connie   That's a good one.

Lolo Carlos	Ang guapo ni Ben. [Ben is very handsome.]
	Lolo Carlos slaps Ben's shoulder.
	Siguro ang daming babaeng humahabol sa 'yo, 'no? [I bet there's a lot of girls chasing after you, right?]
	Ben just smiles politely. Lolo Carlos is disappointed.
	Ano ba yan. Ni hindi marunong magmano o magtagalog. [What's this. Doesn't know how to bless nor understand Tagalog.]
	Roland looks at his plate, biting back an answer.
Tita Connie	These kids today don't have the discipline to learn Tagalog. Look at Jun. All he does is gallivant around with his friends and go disco-disco.
Jun	*(to Rose)* See, told you. Mom's a player hater.
	Stifling a laugh, Rose nudges Jun in the side.
Gina	Would you believe it, Ben? Your cousin Edwin is going to be a lawyer.
Edwin	I'm just majoring in Poli Sci, Tita. Doesn't mean I'm gonna be a lawyer.
Gina	Don't worry, you'll make it. You have your mother's brains.
Tito Lenny	And your father's good looks.
	Tito Lenny strokes his chin and the parents laugh.
Lolo Carlos	So, Ruben, when did you decide to follow your Tito Lenny and become a doctor?
Tito Lenny	Yeah, when was this, Ben?
Roland	I always knew Ben was going into medicine. You know, when he was little, he would bring injured birds home and nurse them back to health.
Tita Connie	If you get sued for malpractice, Edwin can represent you, ha?
	The parents laugh.
Tito Lenny	That scholarship to UCLA is quite an accomplishment, Ben.

Ben Mercado

Rose versus Ben in a friendly game of basketball.

Lolo Carlos holds out his hand for Ben's blessing, but gets a handshake. Rose looks on.

Augusto and his 9 mm

Doug, Ben and Rick at their friend's kegger.

Rose leads her "court" in singkil.

"Happy Birthday" from Gigi, Leslye and Alisha.

At DJ Icy Ice's urging, the Guys step up to the Girls' challenge.

Roland's kundiman (love song)

Annabelle, impressed with Ben's portrait of her.

Ben comes clean with his father.

Tito Lenny turns to Lolo Carlos.

Remember I told you, Pa, nakakuha si Ben ng magandang scholarship para makapasok sa university!
[Ben just received a prestigious scholarship to go to a university.]

Lolo Carlos   *(to Ben)* Yes, that's good. You're a hard worker.

Tita Connie   Oh yes, Ben is a very hard worker. You know, Papa, he also has a full-time job. Jun should learn to be more like him.

Jun   Sorry. I'm too busy going disco-disco.

Tita Connie shoots him a look.

Lolo Carlos   What is this job?

Ben   I work at a comic book store. After school and weekends.

Lolo Carlos   But doesn't that interfere with your studies, Ruben?

Ben   Nah, it's cool. Gotta make money somehow, right?

Lolo Carlos   Hmph. Too bad, ha, Roland?

Lolo Carlos looks over at Roland, who avoids his gaze.

Tita Connie   Ben, didn't you want to go into some art program before?

Ben   Uh, yeah ...

Roland   Oh no. Not anymore. We decided that wasn't a good route for him.

Ben and Rose look at each other.

Tita Connie   Thank God. You'd be one of those bums starving in the streets.

Tito Lenny   By the way, Ben, I talked to my colleague at the hospital. He's willing to bring you on at the front desk of the pediatric ward over the summer.

Tita Connie   You should take advantage of that, Ben. It'll be a good experience for you. Huh, Gina?

Gina half-smiles her approval.

Lolo Carlos   Another doctor will make the family very proud, Ruben.

Tito Lenny	And then Gina and Roland can retire early!
	The parents laugh heartily as Ben gets up from the table.
Ben	Excuse me.
	Hold on Roland watching his son rudely leave as we

Int. Hallway to bath/locker rooms – night

Ben exits the gym floor, rounding a corner into a hallway.

Augusto (o.s.)	So you trying to avoid me now?
Annabelle (o.s.)	Gusto, look…
	Pan over as Ben looks down the hallway. Augusto has his hand on the wall, trapping Annabelle in a corner.
Augusto	Been blowin' up your pager every day. Whussup?
	Annabelle takes a pager out of her purse, gives it back.
Annabelle	Know what? Here, have it. Now stop bothering me.
Augusto	Oh, so it's gonna be like that now.
Annabelle	Look, you're the one who fucked up, so don't you even turn this shit around on me.
Augusto	*(giving the pager back)* Come on, baby, take it. You know how much I paid for that thing.
Annabelle	I don't want it.
Augusto	C'mon, take it.
Annabelle	I said I don't want it!
	Annabelle firmly pushes the pager back to him.
Augusto	Fuck you, then!
	Augusto throws the pager. Annabelle flinches, but it sails past her and smashes against the wall.
Annabelle	Goddammit, Gusto!
	Ben steps up.
Ben	Excuse me. *(they turn to him)* My sister's looking for you.

They both stare at him a moment. Then…

Annabelle	Oh yeah, right. She needs the…the schedule.
Ben	Yeah, the schedule.

Annabelle ducks under Augusto's arm.

Annabelle	Gotta go.

Annabelle takes off down the hallway as Ben and Augusto stare at each other a moment. Then Ben turns to follow her. Track along with Ben and Annabelle.

Ben	Hey! *(Annabelle slows down)* What was that all about?
Annabelle	Just a bunch of dogs, all of you.
Ben	Pleased to meet you, also.
Annabelle	I'm sorry…I didn't mean that. Hi, I'm Annabelle.

She offers a hand. They shake. Side by side like this, Ben notices her easygoing beauty for the first time.

Ben	Yeah, I've seen you hanging with Rose. I'm Ben.
Annabelle	I know. Your sister's told me a lot about you.
Ben	Oh really? How do you know Rose?
Annabelle	We go to State together.
Ben	Oh. So…you're in that dance thing-a-ma-jigger they're doing tonight.
Annabelle	Uhm, yeah. I guess you could call it that.

They stop in front of the door to the Men's Bathroom. An awkward beat.

Well anyway, thanks for helping me out there. I better go get that "schedule" to Rose.

Ben	Yeah. See ya.

He checks her out as she walks away, then turns and walks in the bathroom.

Int. Dinner table – night

A group of Filipino children (ages 5–10) are helping themselves to desserts—kutsinta, puto, sapin sapin, fruit salad, piche piche, all the goodies. Time cut to

Int. Men's Bathroom – night

Ben is at the urinals. Quiet tension as Roland enters and they make awkward eye contact.

Unsure now what to do, Roland goes to the sinks to wash his hands. Ben finishes and goes to the sinks as well.

Ben	I'm not some trophy you can just parade around in front of your whole family.
Roland	What are you talking about? We're proud of you, that's all.
Ben	Be proud of someone else.
Roland	Hay nako. Ba't ba nagkaganito ang buhay ko? [Oh man. How did my life turn out like this?]
Ben	I'm not going to be a doctor.
Roland	I don't believe this hard-headed child. Ruben, we've settled this already.
Ben	We haven't settled anything.
Roland	That cartoon school is a waste of time and money.
Ben	No, med school is a waste of time and money.
Roland	Don't answer back! I am not going to spend $25,000 a year so you can draw those stupid pictures of yours.
Ben	Who asked you to?
Roland	You think you're so smart. You think you know everything. Spoiled is what you are!
Ben	Yeah, right. I'm spoiled.
Roland	Yes, you are spoiled. I've given you everything. *(motions around him)* You don't know what it's like not to have all these things.

Ben	So?
Roland	So I do! I gave my life making sure you don't have to go through what I did! And I'm not going to let you throw that away! Just what the hell do you think you are you going to do in the real world with a degree in cartoons, ha?
Ben	I'm gonna get the hell away from you, that's what.

Ben storms out. Hold on Roland, looking shocked.

Int. Buffet tables – night, continuous

Rose is taking care of business at the buffet tables.

Rose	I think we're running out of rice, Tita.
Tita Florie	I know. The delivery guys brought some extra.

Rose looks over to the

Int. Gym main entrance – night, continuous

Where she sees Ben walking away from the Men's Bathroom. A moment later, Roland comes out and stares at Ben leaving.

Int. Buffet tables – night, continuous

Rose turns to Tita Florie.

Rose	I'll be right back.

Time cut to

Ext. Gymnasium main entrance – night

Ben is talking on a pay phone.

Ben	…I'll be in front of the gym…No, I will not flake out…Just be here, all right?…Yeah, later.

Ben hangs up.

Rose (o.s.)	What are you doing?

Ben stiffens as we angle on Rose walking up behind him.
He doesn't turn to look at her.

Ben   What does it look like?

Rose   Ben, what happened?

Ben turns around to look at his sister.

Ben   Guess.

Rose pauses a beat.

Rose   So you're just gonna leave.

Ben   Sorry, I got better things to do.

Rose   That's your family in there, Ben.

Ben   Yeah, whatever.

Rose stares at him, amazed.

Rose   You actually think you're better than all of us, huh? Just because you hang with white boys and want to study "art" in college, you think you're the shit. Am I right?

Ben   Yeah, so?

Rose is astounded.

Rose   Wake up, little brother. You're just as brown as the rest of us.

She heads back inside. Face darkening, Ben turns to stare out at the parking lot.

Int. Hallway to locker rooms – night

Several traditional dancers are heading for the locker rooms, their costumes draped over their shoulders. Annabelle carries a clipboard and looks stressed out as she walks past them and runs into Rose.

Annabelle   Rose! Have you seen Tito Dante? He's not back yet with the musicians!

Rose   Anna, you gotta mellow out. He's always like this. (*writes on Anna's clipboard*) Here's Tito Dante's cell phone. Call him, see what's up.

Annabelle	I told you, just have a party at Chuck E. Cheese, but nooooo…

Rose laughs as Annabelle scurries off. Then she looks down the hallway and sees Roland standing in the

Int./Ext. Exit door – night, continuous

Roland is silhouetted in the doorway, smoke from his cigarette backlit against the parking lot lights. Rose walks up.

Rose	There you are, Papa, I've been looking all over for you. Tito Dante's not back yet…

Roland turns around, smiles soberly at Rose.

Roland	They're just on Filipino time. I bet you he'll say he lost his keys again.

As Rose pauses a beat, gauging the mood between them, Roland watches a small group of Filipino teenagers hanging out in the parking lot in front of them.

A tricked-out, lowered Acura Integra pulls up to join several more of the teenagers' fixed-up rides, all of which are pulled up in a semi-circle around an asphalt basketball court. On the court, several teenagers are goofing around, shooting baskets.

Rose	Are you okay?
Roland	Yeah, sure.

Roland takes a long drag from his cigarette.

Roland	Don't tell your mom, ha. *(points to the teens)* These kids today, they've got nicer cars than me. *(Rose chuckles)* You know, Rose, I'm not like your Tito Lenny. Or a lot of the other parents.
Rose	Yeah…
Roland	You gotta go to work, go to school. I can't even afford to buy you a decent car.
Rose	Papa, you know that doesn't matter to me.
Roland	I can't even afford a nice debut for you.
Rose	Papa, I told you, I didn't want a debutante ball. This party is more than enough.

Roland smiles at Rose and takes her hand.

Roland I wish your Lola could see you right now. She'd be proud to have a granddaughter as beautiful as you.

Rose smiles warmly. Suddenly, Tito Dante's minivan pulls up, tires squealing as it brakes to a halt.

Tito Dante, Tito Boy and three band members jump out and start grabbing their instruments out of the back.

Tito Dante Sorry I'm late. I misplaced my keys.

Rose and Roland smile at each other knowingly. Time cut to

Int. Backstage – night

Two lines of traditional dancers have gathered, men on one side, women on the other, all chattering excitedly, everyone dressed in various traditional Filipino costumes. Several male dancers are on the ground doing push-ups, pumping their muscles up before they go out in front of everyone. Several female dancers are nervously adjusting each other's costumes.

Track along with Jun and Edwin as they walk down the two lines, slapping low fives with everyone along the way. They reach the head of the line to join Rose, Alisha (18), Gigi (15), and Leslye (19)—"the Girls." They all start pushing Annabelle forward to go onstage.

The Girls You go, girl!

Jun C'mon, Anna, you can do it!

We track with Annabelle as she nervously steps to the

Int. Stage – night, continuous

Annabelle tentatively takes the mic from DJ Icy Ice.

Annabelle   Hello, good evening. My name is Annabelle Manalo, and I'm a friend of Rose. Coming up next we have a special performance by the birthday girl and some of our friends. We've been working on this for a couple of months now, and I think we came up with something really nice. So please take a seat and grab that last piece of chicken adobo, 'cause you don't want to miss it. Maraming salamat po.

Int. Gymnasium – night, continuous

The gym lights dim as the party guests start taking their seats. The photographer and videographer have positioned themselves by the stage, ready to document the event.

Ext. Gym main entrance – night, continuous

Ben is watching Annabelle step offstage. He doesn't notice Doug and Rick sneaking up behind him.

Rick   Ben!!!

Ben jumps up about ten feet. Turns and shoves Rick.

Ben   What the hell, dude!

The guys laugh, then look inside. The dancers are filing onto the dance floor, preparing to start. Rose and Edwin are in the middle of the floor, surrounded by all the other dancers.

The music starts—a Spanish guitar playing a simple but catchy melody.

Doug   What's this?

Ben   Ah, just my sister's birthday dance thing.

Rick   Hey, looks like those Mexican dances my cousins do.

Doug   Who's the belle in white?

Ben   That's my sister.

Doug   Really? She's pretty cute.

Ben stares at him like he's insane.

Ben   We going?

Rick   Wait up a bit, let's check this out.

Rick and Doug go inside. Ben hesitates a moment, then follows them.

Int. Dance floor – night, continuous

Six male and female dancers have lined up in couples along the stage, dressed in tribal costumes and holding costume weapons. Crouching on the floor in front of them are four male dancers manning two pairs of long bamboo poles, positioned in a "V" pattern around Rose and Edwin. Four female dancers have taken their positions outside each pair of poles.

Edwin is circling Rose, symbolically trying to win her affections. He is wearing a barong, a formal, sheer-white Filipino shirt delicately embroidered with intricate traditional patterns. Rose is in a beautiful full-length white lace dress. She twirls a white parasol and keeps him at bay, flirting with her eyes, but not allowing him to come near. Graceful steps. In the background, the tribal dancers along the stage tap their weapons on the ground in time with the music.

The guitar is joined by a drum beat and the metallic gongs of a kulintang. The male dancers kneeling next to the poles begin to clap them against each other and on the floor in rhythm with the music.

Int. Mercado table – night, continuous

Lolo Carlos sits with Roland, Gina, Father Bob, Tito Lenny, Tita Connie and Tita Florie. Roland looks over at his father, who is watching the dance politely.

Int. Dance floor – night, continuous

The bamboo dancers begin to jump in and out of the clapping poles in perfect step, narrowly missing the hard bamboo each time they jump in and out of them.

Rose and Edwin step up and also begin to dance in and around the bamboo. The tribal dancers along the stage start tapping their weapons faster.

Suddenly the music cuts except for a slow beat played by the kulintang. All the dancers stop. Rose and Edwin head to the middle of the floor, and the bamboo dancers don blindfolds. The bamboo clappers move the two pairs of poles into a cross. The crowd murmurs with excitement.

The tribal dancers by the stage each pick up two lit candles in small glass jars, wrap them in sheer handkerchiefs, and hold one in each hand. Soft candlelight flickers around the darkened gym. A tense beat, and the dance begins again.

The music is faster now. The blindfolded bamboo dancers in turn pick up the pace while moving in and out of the clapping poles. Rose, Edwin and the candle/tribal dancers begin to run circles around the bamboo cross.

Int. Gym main entrance – night, continuous

Ben, Doug and Rick watch this difficult display of strength and coordination with genuine amazement. Doug and Rick start tapping their feet and bobbing their heads, caught up in the pure dynamic energy of the dancing.

Int. Dance floor – night, continuous

The candle/tribal dancers start twirling the candles around their bodies, flickering candlelight dancing back and forth across their faces.

Close on the feet the blindfolded bamboo dancers as they jump in and out of the clapping bamboo at incredible speed.

Inserts of the audience loving every minute of the show.

The music builds to a crescendo as the dance finishes in a flurry of twirling bright colors. The lights come back up as the bamboo dancers tear off their blindfolds and raise their hands triumphantly alongside all the other dancers. All the guests get to their feet and cheer wildly in approval.

Int. Mercado table – night, continuous

The entire Mercado family is on its feet cheering. Lolo Carlos, however, is still seated, clapping politely. He slowly gets to his feet to join the rest of the crowd.

Int. Stage, band area – night, continuous

The dancers run over to the band, euphoric, everyone chattering excitedly. The guys are doing some serious male-bonding, high-fiving each other, jumping on each other's backs, adrenaline pumping through them.

Int. Stage – night, continuous

Rose steps onstage and takes the microphone.

Rose So you likes? *(the crowd cheers)* Cool! It's so great to see you all here. We were trying to think of the best way to say thank you to everyone for coming out and celebrating my birthday with me. And this is what we came up with. I just want to take this opportunity to thank all the people that put this party together for me. Mom and Dad, the entire Mercado family clan, Lolo Carlos, who came all the way out here from the Philippines, maraming salamat po…

She smiles warmly at Lolo Carlos. He nods and smiles back.

And thank you to Tito Dante and Tita Florie, all of the awesome dancers and musicians, oh, and last but definitely not least, my good friend, the choreographer of the beautiful dancing you just saw, Annabelle Manalo!

Rose waves at Annabelle to come onstage. She shakes her head shyly. All the dancers cheer and push her forward. Rose drags her onstage and they take a bow. More wild cheers of approval from the crowd, still on its feet.

As Rose and Annabelle step offstage, Edwin and Jun come up and give them two big bouquets of red roses. Annabelle is fighting back tears as the four of them hug tightly.

Int. Gym main entrance – night, continuous

Close on Ben, staring at Annabelle, Rose and the dancers. Almost everyone his age is out on the floor in costume, celebrating. Except for him.

Rick	How come you weren't up there, dude? That shit was cool.
Doug	Wait, let me guess, you had to work.
Rick	Dude works more than a Jamaican and shit.
Doug	*(Jamaican accent)* You so lazy, man. I got five jobs, man!

Ben just looks at Doug and Rick as they laugh and high-five each other. Right then Gina scurries past.

Gina	Hoy, I didn't know you two were here!
Doug	Hi, Mrs. Mercado. We just came to pick up…ah… *(Ben shoots Doug a glare)*…we came to eat.
Gina	Oh, that's good. Now you'll have a chance to taste my cooking. Come! *(drags the two away)* You guys are so skinny. Don't your parents feed you?

Track along with Gina as she pulls Doug and Rick away. Rack focus to Ben being left behind in the background. Time cut to

Int. Stage – night, later

As the DJs put on Billy Ray Cyrus' "Achy Breaky Heart," they look at each other and shrug their shoulders.

Int. Dance floor – night, continuous

Line after line of giddy Filipino parents flood the floor and start doing the "Achy Breaky." Father Bob, now wearing a cowboy hat, boisterously leads one of the lines of dancers. Not something you see every day.

Int. Dinner tables – night, continuous

Ben is sitting alone. Edwin, Jun and Annabelle walk up.

Jun   Whatcha doing here with the old folks?

Ben   Observing how I don't want to be when I get older. *(to Annabelle)* Hey, congratulations on your dance. I like the way you did that with the…

Ben gestures the clapping bamboo. Annabelle beams.

I didn't know you were in charge.

Annabelle   It wasn't all me. Your sister helped a lot.

Doug and Rick saunter up, plates and mouths stuffed with food.

Rick   This is some tasty feed, Ben. Especially this chocolate meat stuff.

Doug   Yeah, no wonder you guys have giant forks and spoons.

Ben   Annabelle, Ed, Jun, this is Doug and Rick, buddies of mine from Jefferson. Doug, Rick, this is Edwin, Jun and Annabelle.

Everyone says "hi" and nods heads at each other.

Edwin   You know, we're all hangin' outside until the real music gets back on. Why don't you guys come on out?

Doug   Cool.

Ben   I don't know, we have to go pretty soon.

Annabelle   Go? The party's just getting started.

Ben   *(shifting uncomfortably)* We have another party to go to. Right, guys?

Rick   *(looking at his watch)* We still got time.

Ben	(staring at his friends) Yeah but we don't, you know, know anybody.
Edwin	It's just us guys from the party.
Jun	And Rose's crew from school.
Annabelle	Come on Ben. Hang out for a while. It'll be fun.

Annabelle smiles at Ben as we

Ext. Basketball courts/parking lot – night

High angle establishing. Looks like this is the place to be if you're young and Filipino on this Saturday night. Several rows of tricked-out Hondas and Acuras are pulled up around a basketball court painted onto the parking lot surface. Dozens of young Pinoys and Pinays (men and women) are hanging out and having a good time.

A 3-on-3 game is being played on the basketball court. The players are stripped down to their T-shirts, the atmosphere is friendly and casual.

As we crane down into the scene, a long caravan of tricked-out cars is cruising into the parking lot, boomin' hip hop music. Like something out of a middle-class version of Billionaire Boys Club, they park in perfect alignment alongside the other tricked-out cars.

As we move through the car rows, we find Edwin, Jun and Annabelle leading Ben, Doug and Rick into the scene. Edwin is cheerfully introducing them to everyone.

Edwin	…and this is Rom, Coco, Winston, Kalika, Jeanne, Jojo, Sheila, Ron, Lynda, Danny, Theresa, Bod, Mabel, Mark, Ken, Efren, Raquel, Rene, Francoise, Janice, Eric…

Doug and Rick are enjoying this, smiling and waving back at everyone. Ben, however, is very nervous. Annabelle notices.

Annabelle	Is something wrong?
Ben	Uh, nah, nothing.

Ext. Car rows – night, continuous

The trunk and doors of Augusto's Integra are open, boomin' rap music. He sits inside while Nestor, Rommel and several "Car Guys" surround him.

Augusto   Yo, check this out.

Augusto reaches under his driver's seat and pulls out a shiny, nickel-plated 9 mm handgun. Everyone's eyes pop out of their heads.

Rommel   Damn, where did you get that?

Augusto   I got it from that crazy nigga Harvey.

Nestor   *(thick Filipino accent)* What is it? A Porty-Pibe?

Rommel   Porty-Pibe. Bitch, that's a nine m-and-m. See that?

Augusto hands it to Rommel and he checks it out expertly. Pulls back the slide, enjoying the satisfying "clank" sound it makes.

Shit's tight.

Nestor   *(yanking it out of Rommel's hand)* Rommel, lemme see.

Rommel   What the fuck! I wasn't finished yet.

Rommel grabs it back. Nestor doesn't let go. They start a tug of war with the gun, like little kids arguing over a toy. Augusto slaps them both in the head and takes the gun back.

Augusto   Gimme that shit. Bitches bust a cap in yourselves.

Augusto sees Basketball Player #1 (Filipino, 18) walking up in back of them and puts the gun back under the seat.

Player #1   *(tossing Augusto the ball)* Hey, you guys got next.

Ext. Pussoy dos circle – night, continuous

Several college guys are gathered around playing pussoy dos, a Filipino version of poker. A pile of money is in the center of their circle. They are finishing up a hand as someone's pager starts beeping. In perfect sync, everyone in the circle grabs for their pagers.

Ext. Front courtside – night, continuous

Annabelle and Ben are kickin' it on the hood of a lowered Civic.

Ben …we used to be real tight. Hung out all the time. But it all changed when high school started. He wanted me to join some Filipino gang called Barracuda or something.

Annabelle *(laughing)* Barkada. *(Ben is clueless)* It's Tagalog. It means the people you hang with, your friends.

Ben They didn't seem too friendly to me. You speak Tagalog?

Annabelle Oo, pluently.

Ben That's wild…anyway, he wanted me to join. I don't know about you, but beating up someone 'cause they look at you funny isn't my thing. He gave me this big guilt trip and we ended up not talking anymore. Then his dad died, and he and his mom moved away.

Annabelle He never talks about his father. It's kinda sad.

Ben That's funny how you and Augusto are together.

Annabelle Actually, we're not really together anymore. I mean, your sister finally made me realize that he is just a two-timing player. He's never gonna change.

Ben Augusto? A player? That guy over there.

Ben points at Augusto on the court playing basketball. Annabelle nods.

Get outta here. When we were kids the only playing he would do was with his Nintendo.

Annabelle *(laughing)* I remember when we first met, he busted out with all the moves. I still remember the first thing he said to me… *(mimicking Augusto)* "Do you know where I can find the nearest baker? 'Cause I want a cutie pie just like you."

Ben *(laughing)* If you think that's funny, my friend Rick likes to flirt by comparing hand size.

Annabelle Oh really? Like how?

Ben points at Annabelle's hands.

Ben	Wow, your hands are really small!

Ben nudges Annabelle to respond and she obliges.

Annabelle	Wow! Really!
Ben	Yeah, look.

Ben places his hand on hers, palm to palm.

Ben	Then you wait for the perfect moment. Look into each other's eyes, and…

Ben clasps hands over Annabelle's and she reacts the same.

Annabelle	That was smooth.

Ext. Car rows – night, continuous

Rose is kicking it with the Girls—Gigi, Leslye and Alisha. Gigi notices Ben and Annabelle flirting with each other, and points to them.

Gigi	Hey, check it out. Looks like we got something going on here.
Rose	Oh my God.
Leslye	Your brother's getting his mack on.
Alisha	Nah, she's getting her mack on.
Rose	They're both getting their mack on!

Ext. Car rows – night, continuous

Edwin, Jun, Doug and Rick are hanging out with two Car Guys. The hood to Car Guy #1's Acura Integra is open. Rick is salivating over the custom engine work.

Car Guy #1	Check this out. I installed a new cam and headers. Twenty-five more horses right there. Shit's got crazy pull, baby.
Rick	You squeezing?
Car Guy #1	Nitrous? Fuck no, this is all throttle.

Rick	I hear you.
Doug	How much did it cost? With the body work and all.
Car Guy #1	About two grand.
Car Guy #2	It's cool though. Because the parents paid for it all.

The Car Guys laugh and pound fists. Edwin shakes his head.

Edwin	I can't believe you guys. Just two more Pinoys selling out to the Man.
Car Guy #2	What?
Jun	*(rolling his eyes)* Oh no.
Edwin	You're just two more brown brothers playing into the hands of the car conspiracy.
Rick	Car conspiracy?
Car Guy #1	What are you talking about?

Edwin looks around the scene, then motions them closer.

Edwin	All right, this is very deep stuff, so you guys gotta peep this careful, okay?

Everyone nods and moves in, except for Jun. He shakes his head and hangs back.

Edwin	Cool. *(pausing, looking around)* You see, the conspiracy is a plan by the man to distract us from the problems of our brown brothers and sisters around the world. They're happy we people of color are wasting our time changing our mufflers and lowering our cars. They don't want us to learn about the war the Philippines had with the United States, or how Mexican and Filipino Americans fought side by side to unionize farm labor…

Rick, Doug and the Car Guys look perplexed.

…Yes, it's true. You guys just don't know because you were too busy adjusting your carburetors and intake valves.

Ext. Front courtside – night, continuous

Ben and Annabelle have moved up real close together now.

Ben   Oh I know, how about back rubs?

Annabelle   That is so old.

Ben   Yeah, but it's a classic. Here… *(motions her to turn around)* You must be really tense from all that choreographing.

She groans good-naturedly, then turns her back to Ben. He starts massaging her.

Ext. Basketball court – night, continuous

Augusto, Rommel and Nestor are walking up court, away from the opposing team, catching their breaths. Rommel points to Ben and Annabelle.

Rommel   Gusto, look at that shit! Bitch-ass punk's got some balls.

Augusto   Motherfucker.

Rommel   Boy wants a foot in his ass. We should rush his shit right now!

Nestor   Why? He's just talking to her.

Rommel   *(slaps Nestor)* Nestor, that ain't no talk action. *(to Augusto)* You need to claim that bitch back like a fuckin' caveman and shit!

Ext. Car rows – night, continuous

Several more teens have gathered around and are listening intently to Edwin.

Edwin   …They don't want you to know about the Filipino veterans who fought for America against the Japanese and never got any benefits. The same Japanese who slaughtered thousands of our people during World War II and are now building these cars you're driving. Why do you want to make your cars go faster anyways? You think you're gonna compete in the Daytona 500? When have you ever seen a Filipino in the Daytona 500?

Car Guy #2   Uh, never?

Edwin	Never. And there never will be. Do you know why?

Edwin grabs his arm, pulls back the sleeve, holds it up to his face for him to see.

'Cause you're brown. They don't want colored people like us infiltrating their sport. *(beat, puts his arm down)* They want us to keep fixin' our cars instead of fixin' ourselves.

Rick	That's deep.
Doug	Wow.

Ext. Basketball court – night, continuous

Augusto makes the winning shot, and he, Rommel and Nestor celebrate their victory.

Rommel	*(to the Car Rows)* Yo! Who's got next?

Time cut to

Ext. Front courtside – night, moments later

Edwin is talking to Rose while he takes off his dress shirt. Gigi, Leslye and Alisha are also hanging out. In the court behind them, Augusto and his crew are shooting warm-up baskets.

Edwin	If you weren't so pretty and all, we'd let you ball with us.
Rose	Golly, Edwin, you're so thoughtful.
Jun	*(running up)* Yo, kuya, I can't get anyone.
Edwin	Damn.

Edwin looks around, then turns to Ben and Annabelle, who are still kickin' it by the Civic.

Yo, Ben! We need a third.

Edwin tosses Ben a basketball. Ben catches it.

Ben	Ed…
Edwin	Come on. Be just like old times, remember?

Rommel and Augusto step courtside, effusing big attitude.

Augusto   Can we get some real ballers in here?

Rommel   Looks like someone doesn't want to be taken to court.

Ben and Augusto's eyes lock. Time cut to

Ext. Basketball court – night, later

Close on Augusto dribbling the ball and talkin' smack to somebody off screen.

Augusto   Still got game, Ruben?

Reverse angle, revealing Ben, iron faced.

Augusto drives for the basket, lowers his shoulder and slams into Ben, who falls down. Augusto lays it in.

Edwin   Dude, flagrant foul!

Augusto triumphantly throws his arms in the air and looks courtside for Annabelle's approval.

Ext. Courtside – night, continuous

Loud protests from the small crowd developing courtside. Rose, Annabelle, Doug, Rick, Leslye, Alisha and Gigi are in the middle of it.

Rose   (*sarcastic*) Wow, weren't you impressed.

Annabelle   (*withering*) Very.

Rick   Yo, Ben, don't take that shit!

Alisha   Yeah, Ben, win it for Annabelle!

Everyone stops and looks at Alisha. An embarrassed Annabelle starts to blush.

Ooops. Sorry.

Ext. Basketball court – night, continuous

Edwin is getting in Augusto's face.

Edwin   What the hell was that?

Augusto shoves Edwin away.

Augusto   You got a problem with that, nigga?

Edwin   No, I don't, Pinoy…

Ben gets up in between them.

Ben   Don't worry about it, it's cool.

Rommel grabs Augusto and pulls him backcourt. Augusto manages one last shove to Ben's head.

Augusto   No bitches allowed on my court.

Series of tightly edited shots—fast, acrobatic play from both teams. Lots of outside shots from long range, balls being swatted down. Very physical defense, hard body checks, pushing and shoving. A heavy hardcore beat pounds on the soundtrack. Time cut to

Ext. Courtside – night, later

Annabelle   Score?

Rose   Game point, 6–6.

Ext. Basketball court – night, continuous

Rommel checks the ball to Jun, who passes to Ben. Augusto is immediately all over him, body-checking hard.

Augusto   Let's go punk.

Ben   Is that all you can say?

Augusto   No, bitch.

By the key, Edwin is wide open. Waves his arms up.

Edwin   Ben, drop the bomb!

Ben ignores him. Augusto is covering Ben like a blanket. Ben drives to the hole.

Augusto Don't even think you can bust one on me, white boy.

Ben is taken aback and loses control of the ball. Augusto steals it and makes an easy lay up for the win.

Ext. Courtside – night, continuous

Mixed cheers from the crowd. The Girls are bummed. Rick taps Doug on the shoulder and points to his watch.

Titas Connie and Florie step up to Rose and the Girls.

Tita Florie Hoy! Rose, tell everyone to come inside.

Tita Connie It's time to cut the birthday cake.

Rose Oh okay. Sorry, Tita.

She turns and yells out to everyone in a fake Filipino accent.

Hoy! You kids, it's time por de birtday cake! Ebrybody inside!

Tita Connie points to the court area with her lips.

Tita Connie Why do you have to party over here when there's a party over there?

Ext. Basketball court – night, continuous

Augusto, Nestor and Rommel are slapping hands with several Car Guys, enjoying their victory. Augusto glares at Ben.

Ext. Courtside – night, continuous

Ben, Edwin and Jun are walking off the court, putting their party clothes back on.

Jun Damn, we could've schooled those punks. I can't believe you lost that handle.

Ben is silent, dejected. Edwin notices.

Edwin	Man, don't listen to him. You know, Ben, it's a little known fact that pound for pound, Filipinos are the best basketball players in the world.
Jun	Too bad we're all only five foot six.
Edwin	So what? Look at Mugsy Bogues. He's Filipino. He just doesn't want to admit it. That nose of his is straight up mountain province.

Doug, Rick and Rose walk up.

Rick	Hey, I think we gotta get going.
Edwin	Ah, serious?
Doug	We gotta get to the other party.
Edwin	All right, then, check you guys later.

They all exchange handshakes.

Rose	Nice meeting you.
Rick	Same here.
Doug	Happy birthday.
Rose	Thanks. I'll see you guys soon.

Rose, Edwin and Jun head for the gym. Ben hangs back.

See you inside, Ben?

Ben	Yeah…I'll be there in a minute.

Doug and Rick look at Ben curiously.

Doug	Dude, you all right?
Rick	Relax, man, you'll forget the whole thing when we get to Sheldon's. *(no reaction from Ben)* You still want to go, right?
Doug	If you want, we can hang 'til they cut the cake. Up to you.

Ben looks back to the court and sees Augusto with his arm around Annabelle. They're walking back to the gym together. He turns back at the guys.

Ben	Let's go get fucked up.

Ben, Doug and Rick head for the Mustang.

Ext. Courtside – night, continuous

Annabelle is obviously not enjoying Augusto's attention.

Annabelle   Gusto, get your arm off of me.

Augusto notices Ben leaving with Doug and Rick.

Augusto   Looks like the chump can't hang.

Annabelle   What is wrong with you? Why do you have to be such an asshole all the time?

Augusto   Babe, c'mon, why you trippin'?

Augusto tries to pull her closer to him.

Annabelle   I'm not your babe. Get the hell away from me!

She heads for the gym. Augusto stares at her walking away.

Ext. Rick's Mustang – night, continuous

Ben is musing in the back seat as Rick starts up his Mustang.

Rick   Time to get ripped, dudes!

Doug   Hey, I got my brother's ID. Let's stop by a liquor store on the way.

Rick   Right on.

Ben isn't paying attention. He turns around to look back at the gym as Rick starts pulling out of the parking lot.

Ext. Gym main entrance – night, continuous

Edwin and Rose are watching them drive away, disappointed. Rose steps forward and catches Ben's look.

Ext. Rick's Mustang – night, continuous

Close on Ben as he quickly turns back around, ashamed.

Rick   Dude, let's get some Boone's!

Doug   Yeah! That stuff fucks you up.

Ext. Sheldon's house – night

Low angle establishing. Alternative rock music is blasting from this upper-middle-class home. Cars are jammed onto its driveway and lawn, various white teenagers are partying in the front yard. The garage door is open to the inside where there is a keg and more partying teens.

Move in as Ben, Doug and Rick walk up to the garage, their backs to the camera. They slap high fives with the partygoers as they enter.

Int. Den – night, continuous

Except for a couple of card tables and a few folding chairs, all the furniture has been moved out of the room. In the darker corners of the space we catch glimpses of couples making out, kids puffing weed, etc.,

Several teenagers surround Doug, Rick, Ben, Jennifer and Susie, who are seated at a card table. They are playing "I Never," a "Truth or Dare"–like drinking game. Everyone is tipsy and happy; a very drunk Susie drinks greedily from a Big Gulp.

Susie Fuck these lame questions. Let's get to the juicy stuff.

Ben Oh? And what would that be?

Susie You know. Here, I'll start you off. I never…had sex.

All eye each other curiously. Rick nervously adjusts his collar.

Rick Oh come on. That's too easy.

Susie Come on. Who's green here…

Doug and Jennifer seem unsure of themselves.

Hey, I better not be the only one drinking.

One by one, everyone takes a drink.

Susie All right, then how about…I never masturbate. *(only she drinks)* Oh come on. That's bullshit. I know all of you do it.

Jennifer I don't.

Susie   Yeah, right.

Ben nudges Rick and nods towards Doug. They smile mischievously and drink.

Doug   Really, guys? Wow.

Ben   C'mon, Douglas.

Rick   Can't lie, bro.

Doug   *(taking a sip)* Okay, okay, okay.

Ben and Rick burst out laughing and slap high fives.

Ben   Sorry, dude. We were just kidding.

Doug   Fuck you!

Rick   So what is it, an everyday thing for you? Or once a week. Baywatch Nights, right?

Ben   Sorry, Doug, no more handshakes for you.

Rick   *(grabbing Doug's hand)* Lemme see those hairs on your palm.

Doug   *(yanking his hand away)* Fuck you guys, man.

Everyone laughs. Ben pats Doug on the shoulder good-naturedly.

Ben   Okay, okay, next one.

Rick   Hey, I got a nasty one for the girls. How about…I never swallowed.

The guys are surprised as Susie proudly drinks from her Big Gulp. Jennifer tries to hide her disgust.

Ben   So, Susie. Got any plans tomorrow night?

Susie   Fuck you, dweeb.

Ben   I'm free after seven!

The guys laugh and slap high fives. Susie glares at Ben.

Susie   All right then. I've got one for you. I never ate a dog.

The girls laugh. When Jennifer sees that Ben isn't laughing, she quiets down.

Oh, I'm sorry. I never ate a cat!

Ben looks down at his drink.

Rick   Hey, that's not cool.

Susie   So? All those Orientals do it.

Susie starts making catcalls at Ben, who sits silent, thoroughly embarrassed.

Jennifer   Susie, come on. That's mean.

Doug   Yeah, Ben's not like that.

Giggling, Susie takes another gulp from her drink.

Rick   Maybe you should mellow on that stuff.

Susie   What're you, my Daddy?

Doug   *(reaching for Susie's drink)* Hey, Susie, can I try some of that?

Susie   No, you can't.

Ben tries to pull the drink out of her hand.

Ben   Why don't you let me hold that for you?

Susie   Let go!

She yanks the cup back to her, popping the lid off and spilling vodka and Orange Gatorade all over her pants.

Fuck! Look what you did! *(stands up)* Look at me! I'm soaked! You fuckin' chink!

Everyone stares at Susie as she tries to wipe herself dry. After a beat…

Ben   I'm not Chinese.

Susie   Yeah, whatever.

Suddenly, Susie's torso jerks violently. A mouthful of vomit splatters on the table.

Rick   What the fuck?!

Doug   Damn…

Susie slaps her hand over her mouth, to no avail. More chunky orange liquid squirts out between her fingers. Everyone scoots away from the table.

Susie finishes unloading all over the table and floor. Rick and Jennifer come to her side.

Rick   You okay?

Jennifer   Come on, Susie, let's go.

Still keeled over and dry-heaving, Susie pushes Rick away, embarrassed.

Jennifer   It's okay, Rick, I've got her.

Jennifer drags her off to the bathroom. Rick is left behind with Doug and several other gawking teens. Ben turns and leaves.

Doug   Hey, Ben, where you going?

Rick   Not only can she swallow, she also chucks up.

Ext. Sheldon's living room – night, continuous

The party is raging on. A mosh pit has formed and dozens of white teens are jumping up and down in unison to a hard alternative rock song. The stereo is blaring.

Close angle on Ben as he moves into frame. He looks lost, packed like a sardine among all the dancing partygoers, looking desperately for the exit.

Ben's P.O.V. as he is buffeted back and forth among the dancing teens. Every single face he sees is White.

Finally, Ben breaks free from the crowd, finds the door, and heads out into the dark street. Time cut to

Ext. Sheldon's house – night

We are looking at the front of Sheldon's house. Track over to reveal Ben sitting on the trunk of Rick's Mustang, staring out into the dark street.

The revelry continues unabated behind him, somewhat out of focus. We can loosely pick out several partygoers peeing on a tree, others vomiting in the bushes, a couple making out on the hood of a car, etc.,

Behind Ben a silhouetted figure walks up and sits down beside him. Doug hands Ben a can of beer. Ben doesn't look at him, simply opens it and takes a sip.

They sit and drink for a while in silence. Eventually…

Doug   We should've never come here. Fucking Rick. *(mimicking Rick)* "Dude, let's get some Boone's Farm. Dude, it's gonna be a rager." Rager! How many people do you know still use that word?

Ben remains silent. Doug puts his arm around Ben.

Forget it, Ben. Crazy bitch was fucked up. She didn't know what she was saying.

Ben finally looks at Doug.

Ben   Yeah, she did.

Doug is speechless. A beat. Ben looks back out to the street.

You up for some cake and ice cream?

Over Ben's closeup, we dissolve to

Int. Mercado family table – night

Ben's closeup dissolves into a closeup of Rose, who is smiling at something offscreen. A birthday song is heard over the DJ's speakers in the background. Annabelle moves into frame.

Annabelle   So what do you think?

Rose   This is too sweet.

Int. Gym, stage – night, continuous

Close on Alisha, Gigi and Leslye singing an original birthday song. Pull out to reveal they are onstage on the microphone, singing to Rose. The videographer and photographer are at the base of the stage, recording.

Int. Gym main entrance – night, continuous

Ben, Doug and Rick arrive. They look around the gym, wondering what to do with themselves.

Int. Uncles' table – night, continuous

Tito Dante, Roland and Tito Lenny are hanging out, having a drink. Tito Lenny puts his arm around Dante.

Tito Lenny   You know, Dan, I think it's time for us to hear a song.

Tito Dante   I think you're right, Lenny.

Int. Stage – night, continuous

The Girls complete their song and the crowd applauds.

Leslye   Happy birthday, Rose.

Alisha   May all your wishes come true.

The Girls   We love you.

The Girls step down and the Crowd ahhhhhs. DJ Icy Ice takes the mic.

DJ Icy Ice   Up next we have a special treat for all of you. The father of the birthday girl is going to sing a song for us! Accompanying Roland are his old bandmates from the Philippines…So take your seats 'cause you're not gonna wanna miss this.

Int. Gym, dinner tables – night, continuous

Dozens of party guests take their seats in anticipation.

Int. Lolos' table – night, continuous

Lolo Carlos is drinking San Miguel beer with Lolo Fred (70s) and Father Bob as he hears the announcement. He shoots a hard glare over to the

Int. Stage – night, continuous

Roland walks uneasily onstage and confers briefly with Tito Dante, who has planted himself behind the DJ's synthesizer.

Roland takes the mic and taps it to check if it's on.

Roland   Hi, everyone. I haven't done this in a while, so please bear with me. This song is dedicated to the two loveliest women in the world—my wife Gina, and my daughter Rose.

Int. Mercado family table – night, continuous

Embarrassed, Rose leans over to Gina and whispers in her ear.

Int. Stage – night, continuous

Tito Dante fires up the synthesizer, and Roland nervously starts to sing a classic Tagalog ballad.

Int. The Guys' table – night, continuous

Edwin, Jun and all the male dancers ("the Guys") are munching on Rose's birthday cake, watching the show at a table next to the dance floor.

Ben, Doug and Rick pull up chairs at their table. Edwin glares at Ben, who sheepishly smiles back at his cousin.

Int. Stage – night, continuous

Even though he started out nervously, Roland's romantic old stage persona starts coming back—strong, self-assured and, yes, sexy.

Int. Mercado family table – night, continuous

Gina grabs Rose and pulls her offscreen. Pan over to Annabelle as she watches them leave.

Int. The Guys' table – night, continuous

Tito Lenny takes a seat at the Guys' table and pours a drink.

Int. Gym – night, continuous

Series of shots around the scene. The crowd is completely into Roland's performance. Couples of all ages are dancing while the videographer, photographer and Tita Connie snap pictures. Older couples are snuggling up close, getting into the romantic mood. Even some of the small children (4–8) at the party have stopped playing to watch the show.

Int. Stage – night, continuous

The crowd breaks into applause as Roland brings Gina and Rose onstage and starts singing to them!

Int. Lolos' table – night, continuous

Lolo Carlos is staring coldly at Roland singing.

Int. Stage – night, continuous

Roland sees Lolo Carlos' glare and coolly turns his back on him.

Then he takes Rose's hand as he hits one final, sweet note to end the song. Rose pretends to faint into Gina's arms, and the entire gym applauds heartily.

Roland gives the microphone back to DJ Icy Ice.

DJ Icy Icy   Give it up for Mr. Roland Mercado! That was tight!

Int. The Guys' table – night, continuous

The whole table is on its feet clapping and cheering.

Jun   Tito Roland! Straight up pimpin'!

Rick   I don't know what the hell he said, but your dad's the bud! *(starts whistling)* Go, Mr. Mercado!

Doug   So, Ben, do all Filipinos party like this?

Rick   Make us Mexicans look Amish and shit.

Ben just looks at his friends, completely surprised.

Doug   *(to Tito Lenny)* Whatever happened to his band?

Tito Lenny contemplates his answer a moment.

Tito Lenny   Well, you know how it is in that business. It's very difficult. Same as here.

Tito Lenny puts his arm around Ben and gives him a warm squeeze.

But then some more important things came along, hah, Ben? *(to Doug and Rick)* After Ben's mom and dad had him, he gave it up and brought them all here to the United States.

Hold on Ben, embarrassed as he watches Roland, Gina and Rose by the

Int. Gym, dance floor – night, continuous

Surrounded by party guests, Tita Connie is taking the Mercados' picture in front of the stage.

Int. Stage – night, continuous

DJ Icy Ice   *(on the mic)* So is there anybody else with a dedication for Rose? *(no answer from the crowd)* I guess that's it.

Int. Mercado family table – night, continuous

Blushing, Rose sits down next to Annabelle, who gives her a big hug.

Annabelle   That was so cute!

Rose   Oh God, I'm totally embarrassed.

Ben *(o.s.)*   Excuse me.

Offscreen, Ben gets onstage. Annabelle spots this.

Annabelle   Rose…

She points to the stage. Rose turns around and sees

Int. Stage – night, continuous

Ben steps up to Ice and puts his hand out for the mic. Takes it, then nervously turns to the crowd.

Int. Vasquez/Johnson table – night, continuous

Augusto, Rommel and Nestor are guzzling fruit punch and munching on chicharones dipped in vinegar. All three have noticeably bloodshot eyes. Rommel spots Ben heading onstage and points him out to Augusto.

Rommel   Hey, yo yo yo! The bitch is back!

Augusto   Motherfucker.

Nestor   *(oblivious)* Could you please pass the vinegar?

Int. Stage – night, continuous

Ben tentatively steps to the front of the stage with the mic.

Ben   Hi. So, um, if some of you don't know me, I'm Rose's brother Ben. I don't have a long speech or anything. I guess all I really want to say is…sorry, Rose.

Int. Mercado table – night, continuous

Move in slow on Rose as Ben gives his speech.

Ben   *(cont.)* I really am sorry for not being there for you these past couple of months. You're the coolest sis any guy can have, and you deserve better…Yeah, that's all. Happy birthday, Rose.

End on a tight close up of Rose as she smiles at her brother.

Int. Gym, dance floor – night, continuous

The crowd applauds politely. Roland, Gina and Tito Lenny smile warmly at each other as Ben walks off stage.

In the background, the DJs finally start playing modern dance music as we make a time cut to

Int. Stage – night, continuous

DJ Icy Ice   *(on the mic)* All right, guys, it's about time to set things off! Representin' on the turntables, my home boy, DJ E-Man. And I'm DJ Icy Ice on the m–i–c. Let's see you all grab a partner, get on up and dance!

Int. The Girls' table – night, continuous

Annabelle, Rose, Gigi, Alisha and the rest of the Girls are kicking it. Leslye walks up and points to the Guys' table across the way.

Leslye   So we gonna go groove, girls?

Annabelle	You guys can go. I think I'm just gonna chill for a little.
Gigi	Oh come on, Anna.
Rose	Why don't you ask Ben to dance with you?
Annabelle	Yeah, right. With Gusto here?
Rose	Anna…
Leslye	Hello, aren't you, like, not with him?
Annabelle	But he might get mad.
Alisha	Mad? Excuse me, but remember what he's done to you?
Leslye	He doesn't own you.
Gigi	Yeah, forget that misogynistic colonial bullcrap.

Surprised, everyone just looks at Gigi. Rose turns to the Guys' table and waves at Edwin.

Int. The Guys' table – night, continuous

Edwin sees Rose waving at him. She very obviously points to Annabelle. Edwin nods and leans over to Ben, who is talking to Rick.

Ben	A sketch?
Rick	Dude, she'll dig it.
Edwin	Hey, Ben, I think Annabelle wants you to ask her to dance.

Ben looks at Edwin curiously.

Int. The Girls' table – night, continuous

Annabelle is thoroughly embarrassed.

Annabelle	What are you doing?
Rose	Oh my gosh, looks who's coming.

Annabelle turns and sees Ben walking up. She quickly turns back around, mortified.

Annabelle	No, you didn't!

Rose	Yes, I did.
Annabelle	I'm gonna kill you, Rose.
	Ben steps up to Annabelle.
Ben	Hey.
Annabelle	Hi.
Alice (o.s.)	Come, Ben! Time to dance!

Like a tornado Alice swoops in from behind, grabs Ben and starts dragging him to the dance floor.

Ben shoots a pleading look at an amused Annabelle. Time cut to

Int. Stage/dance floor – night

Ice takes control of the party and slips into MC mode.

DJ Icy Ice	All right party people, I don't see enough empty seats out there. Don't be shy—girls grab a guy, guys grab a girl! Let's get this party started right!

Most of the older parents have cleared away as the younger generation takes over the floor.

A line of dancers has formed—girls on one side, guys on the other. Couples dance down the aisle in turn, showing off their moves. Don Cornelius would be proud.

A boisterous Alice drags Ben down the line with her. He's trying to be cool about the situation, but the Guys aren't making things any easier for him.

Edwin	Bust a move, Ben!
Jun	Wax that booty!

Ben smiles dryly and scratches his forehead with his middle finger.

Next in line is Doug dancing awkwardly down the line with Rose.

Int. Mercado family table – night, continuous

Gina and the Titas are laughing at Rose and Doug.

Tita Florie   Hoy! Tingnan n'yo si Rose, kasama niya yung puti!
[Look at Rose with that white guy!]

Gina   Totoo ng hindi sila marunong sumayaw!
[It's true. They can't dance!]

Beside them are Roland and the Titos trying to copy one of the dance moves they see the kids doing. In the middle of the move, Tito Lenny strains his back and has to take a seat.

Int. Stage/dance floor – night, continuous

Boom! A funky bass groove thunders across the gym. Banks of disco lights start flashing all around the dance floor. Ice hits the mic again.

DJ Icy Ice   All right, told y'all we'd get you hyped! DJ E-Man! Master turntablist on the wheels of steel!

DJ E-Man hunkers down and starts scratching. The Soul Train line breaks up and the dancers start freestyling.

Ben spots Annabelle dancing with Alisha, Gigi and Leslye in the middle of the dance floor. He starts toward her, but runs into Doug and Rick, who are being pushed back as an empty circle starts to open up.

In the circle, Annabelle and the Girls are in the middle of a perfectly coordinated dance routine. Their moves are fresh, many based on the traditional Filipino dances we saw earlier.

Attitude flowing, Jun and three male dancers step up to the girls and watch their routine, unimpressed.

Watching by the perimeter, Ben, Doug and Rick are amazed. Janet Jackson's got nothing on this.

The Girls end their routine and stare the Guys down, daring the fellas to outdo them. The crowd cheers, completely into the moment.

DJ Icy Ice	Uh oh, looks like we got a battle brewing here! Fellas, you gonna take that? Let's show these ladies it's a man's world!

Rose, Annabelle and the Girls let out a collective amiable groan and wave Ice off. Jun and the Guys step up to the challenge and throw down their own routine.

Int. Lolos' table – night, continuous

Lolo Carlos, Lolo Fred, Father Bob and Lola Carmen (80's) watch the goings-on, laughing at all the funny dance moves.

Int. Stage/dance floor – night, continuous

The Guys wrap up their routine and stare down the Girls, inciting equally loud cheers from the Crowd.

DJ Icy Ice	I don't know, party people, that looked like a tie to me. E-Man, break us off another beat!

As DJ E-Man effortlessly mixes into a new jam, Jun and Annabelle spontaneously break into the cha-cha! The energy is infectious as everyone around them starts to follow their lead. Even Doug and Rick pair up with partners! Ben makes his way over to Annabelle.

Ben	Hi.
Annabelle	Hey, you! Didn't know you were into older women.
Ben	Well, when you got it, you got it. *(to Jun)* Can I cut in?
Annabelle	Do you know how to cha-cha?
Ben	No, but I can try.

Int. Gym, bleachers – night, continuous

Augusto and Rommel are watching the dancers, trying to look hard. Nestor is playing with the balloons behind them. Rommel notices Ben stepping to Annabelle.

Rommel	Damn, nigga just doesn't learn.

Augusto stares at Ben and Annabelle, seething.

Augusto Punk motherfucker.

Rommel *(right in Augusto's face)* What the fuck you waiting for?

Nestor Hey, guys, look at this.

Nestor has taken one of the balloons and let the air out in his mouth.

My voice sounds funny now.

Int. Stage/dance floor – night, continuous

Jun graciously steps aside as Annabelle takes Ben's hands, leading him in an impromptu cha-cha lesson. Ben starts out a little awkwardly.

Annabelle Try it again. One, two, cha-cha-cha. Three, four, cha-cha-cha. Work those hips!

Ben This is a lost cause.

Annabelle Come on, if you're Filipino you can cha-cha. It's in your blood.

She steps up behind him, takes his arms and guides him. Ben smiles, enjoying being close to Annabelle like this. They try the dance again. Much better.

You got it.

Ben I do?

Seeing the two of them so close together, all the guys and girls around them start ooohing and aaahing, good-naturedly cheering them on.

Int. Side of dance floor – night, continuous

A group of children (4–8) have formed a little circle and are bustin' moves. Lolo Carlos comes up and throws a big handful of change in the air. As it rains down on the kids they scramble on the ground to pick it up. The photographer and videographer are on hand to capture the adorable sight.

Int. Dance floor – night, continuous

Series of shots around the dance floor showing that just about everyone at the party has now paired up and is doing a mean cha-cha.

Close on Ben as the sheer communal joy of the moment loosens him up and he starts improvising, spinning in circles and twirling Annabelle around as well. A Cha-Cha King in the making. Dissolve to

Int. Gymnasium – night, later

High angle. The gym has cleared out as the party is winding to a close. Gina and the Titas are giving leftovers to the departing guests. The DJs have a mellow R&B jam playing in the background while they pack their equipment. Father Bob, Lolo Fred and Lola Carmen are saying their goodbyes to Lolo Carlos at the main entrance. Some of the dancers are helping clean up, garbage bags in hand.

Ext. Gym dumpster area – night, continuous

Garbage bags in hand, Ben and Annabelle walk up to the trash dumpsters behind the gym.

Ben	There were so many people tonight. I didn't even know who I was related to.
Annabelle	That's the scary thing about these parties. You don't know who's family sometimes.
Ben	Wait, we're not related, are we?
Annabelle	Ah, no. Definitely not.
Ben	Phew. Good.

Ben reaches into his jacket and pulls out the napkin he was drawing on earlier.

Say, um, I made something for you.

Annabelle	Really? What?

	Ben modestly hands Annabelle the napkin. She opens it. It's a beautiful drawing of her profile. Annabelle's jaw drops.
Rommel (o.s.)	Whussup, nigga!
	Ben and Annabelle turn to see Augusto leading Rommel and Nestor.
Ben	Shit.
Augusto	Got it hard for my girl, punk?
Annabelle	Gusto, don't…
Augusto	Shut up, ho! You think you can replace me with this bitch-ass punk?
	Augusto shoves Ben back, then gets right up in his face like a baseball manager yelling at an umpire. Ben holds his ground.
	Bitch! Why you mad doggin' me?
Ben	What are you talking about?
Annabelle	Gusto, stop!
Rommel	Nigga, don't even play Gump on us. You practically shoved your dick down her throat!
Ben	I don't want any trouble, okay, Augusto?
	Augusto pushes him again, even harder.
Augusto	Fuck you, white boy.
Ben	I'm not a white boy.
Augusto	Oh yeah? Who do you hang with that ain't white? *(no response from Ben)* Yeah, see, you've always been a fuckin' sell out. *(shove)* Come on, pussy. *(shove)* See what you got. *(shove)* Fuckin' white boy! *(shove)* Fuckin' coconut!
	Crack! Ben clocks Augusto a solid right across his jaw. Augusto stumbles back.
Rommel	Ah, shit!
Nestor	Hay, nako!
	Augusto dives at Ben, tackling him hard down to the ground. They break loose on each other, twisting around, tearing at

each other's clothes, slapping, kicking, punching. A real dirty street brawl. Annabelle runs inside to get help.

Rommel   Fuck 'em up, D! Yeah, yeah! Take his shit out!

Neither one can get up, each clawing the other down when the other tries to stand. Nestor is agitated as he watches the fight, looking all around, not knowing what to do. Rommel, on the other hand, circles Ben and Augusto as they twist around on the ground, taunting them on, kicking Ben down when he tries to get up.

Suddenly, Rommel is tackled by Edwin! Jun shoves Nestor to the side as Tito Lenny and Roland jump on bloodied Augusto and Ben and pry them apart.

The remaining party guests (all the main characters) rush out of the gym. Tito Lenny holds Ben around the chest, trying to pull him away from Augusto, who is held by Roland. Ben manages one last kick to Augusto's torso. Roland curses in Tagalog.

Roland   Ruben! Stop that!

Augusto   Motherfuckin' punk bitch!

Ben   Fuck you!

Augusto   Fuckin' sell out white boy! I'm gonna fuck your shit up!

Roland tightens his hold around Augusto.

Roland   Hey! Calm down now!

Augusto   C'mon bitch, I'll take your ass out, right now!

Ben   Let's go then, you fuck!

Tito Lenny   You two stop it now!

As Augusto struggles to break free, Roland feels something on him.

Roland   Hoy! What is this?

He puts Augusto in a headlock, reaches down into his back waistband and pulls out Augusto's handgun! Everyone suddenly freezes, shocked. Tito Lenny lets go of Ben, who no longer struggles against him.

What the hell are you doing with this thing, goddammit?

Augusto	Yo! Gimme back my shit!

Augusto tries to grab the gun away from Roland, who holds it beyond his reach and gives it to Edwin.

Roland	Were you planning to use it? Hah?
Augusto	Fuck you, man!

Furious, Roland tightens his grip, practically strangling Augusto.

Roland	Big shot with a gun, hah? Hah?!

Suddenly Roland gets a hard smack upside the head from Alice! He lets go Augusto, who falls to the ground, gasping for air.

Alice	Hoy! [What are you doing? What is wrong with you?!]

She goes after Roland, screaming Tagalog curses like a banshee, slapping him repeatedly. Roland holds his arms up, shielding himself from Alice's hits.

Roland	Alice! [Stop! Stop it! Wait a minute!]

George grabs his hysterical wife, restraining her.

George	Alice! Calm down!
Alice	[You bastard! What are you doing to my son?!]

Roland takes the now-unloaded gun from Edwin and shows it to Alice. Her feral eyes stare at the weapon, refusing to comprehend. Behind her, George is mortified and lets her go.

What is that? Where did you get that?!

Roland	Your son, Alice! Your son brought a gun to our party!

Angle on Augusto slowly getting to his feet.

George	Jesus Christ…
Alice	What are you talking about? What are you doing with that?
Roland	I got it from that boy of yours!
Alice	Shut up! That's not his! You're lying!

Roland	He could have killed somebody with this!
Alice	That's not his gun! It's those hooligan friends of his!

Alice points over to Rommel and Nestor in the corner. George shakes his head in utter disbelief.

George	Oh my God, Alice...
Alice	It's not his gun. It's his friends' gun! Look at him, he's a good boy!
George	Alice! Would you wake up and stop being so goddamn naïve?! Face it, your son's a gangbanger!

Augusto jumps forward and shoves George back.

Augusto	Shut the fuck up! Don't you ever talk to her like that again, you hear me? You fuckin' hear...

Alice whacks Augusto in the head.

Hey!

Alice	Tama na! Don't disrespect your father!

As Alice slaps Augusto again we angle on Ben watching the chaos.

Augusto (o.s.)	Fuck, Ma!

Move past him to Lolo Carlos, who shakes his head in disgust.

Alice (o.s.)	Shut up! What are you doing talking like that? Ay susmaryosep, you're such a rude boy!

Extreme close-up of Ben's napkin drawing of Annabelle, crumpled on the cold concrete.

Ext. Gym back entrance – night, later

As Tita Connie, Tita Florie and Tito Dante load the empty metal food trays back into Tita Florie's minivan, they discreetly look out to the

Ext. Parking lot – night, continuous

George and Alice, both humiliated, pull out of the lot in George's Lincoln Continental. Augusto fumes quietly in the back. They leave frame to reveal

Ext. Parking lot, Rommel's Integra – night, continuous

Rommel is urinating onto a row of bushes. Nestor is nervously standing behind him, in front of Rommel's Integra.

Rommel   I can't believe your bitch ass just stood there! At least I got my kicks in.

Nestor   But it wouldn't be pair.

Rommel   What did you say?

Nestor   It wouldn't be pair to jump in.

Rommel   Pair? What the fuck does fruit have to do with this? I can't believe you're fuckin' related to me! Been here two fuckin' years and still you talk like you went through customs yesterday! I swear, you tired ass FOB's come to this country and make the rest of us look stupid.

Nestor   Stop calling me a FOB.

Rommel   What are you gonna do about it, fresh off the boat motherfucker?

Nestor winds up and punches Rommel hard in the face, sending him flying back against Augusto's car.

Int. Gymnasium, bleachers – night, continuous

Close on Ben as Gina and Rose tend to his cuts and bruises with a first aid kit. Even though the gym is now all but empty, tension is thick in the air.

Lolo Carlos (o.s.)   …Ang tigas kasi ng ulo mo! Hindi ka nag-iisip! Irresponsable! [I can't believe how hard-headed you are! You don't think! So irresponsible!]

We move past Gina, Rose and Ben to the

Int. Gym main entrance – night, continuous

Tito Lenny stands beside Roland, who is being berated by an enraged Lolo Carlos. They are arguing just around the corner from the bleachers where Ben, Rose and Gina are sitting.

Lolo Carlos   (cont.) At ba't ka nag-iimbita ng mga barumbadong tao dito? Pinabayaan mo lang ang mga hoodlums na 'yon! Halos mapatay pa nila'ng apo ko!
[And how could you invite those kinds of people? Letting hoodlums like that in here! Almost got my grandson killed!]

Tito Lenny   'Tay, tama na 'yan...
[Pa, that's enough...]

Roland   Kaibigan namin ang magulang ng mga batang 'yon. I didn't expect this to happen...
[Those kids' parents are friends of ours.]

Lolo Carlos   You didn't expect because you didn't think! Anong klaseng magulang ka? Masyado ka kasing pasikat! Kung hindi mo inunang magpakanta-kanta, hindi mangyayari ito! Wala ka na bang respeto sa sarili mo? Nakakahiya ka talaga! Ikinahihiya ka ng pamilyang ito!
[What kind of parent are you, anyway? If you weren't so busy gallivanting around on that stage like a big shot, this wouldn't have happened! Don't you have any self-respect? You make me so ashamed! You're an embarrassment to this family!]

Roland hangs his head and stares at the ground.

Tito Lenny   'Tay, huminahon na kayo.
[Pa, calm yourself.]

Lolo Carlos   Kung nakinig ka lang sa sinasabi ko sa iyo noon pa, hindi lang ito ang mararating mo. Pakantakanta...ano bang narating mo sa kalokohang iyon? Wala! Ano ka ngayon? Kartero! Taga-hatid ng sulat. Hindi ka makabuhay ng sarili mong pamilya. Ni sarili mong anak nga hindi mo mabigyan ng maayos na debut. Kung hindi dahil sa kapatid mo, lalong wala ka ngayon. Siguro pulubi ka nang pakalat-kalat d'yan sa kalye!

[If you only listened to what I was telling you over and over again, you could have been somebody. Fooling around on stage…What has that foolishness brought to you? Nothing! So what are you now? A postman! Delivering people's mail. You can barely provide for your own family! Can't even afford to give your only daughter a proper debutante ball! If it wasn't for your brother taking care of you, you'd be nothing but a bum on the streets!]

Tito Lenny   Tay, ano ba iyan? Sinabi nang tumigil na kayo! Hindi ninyo ba kayang manahimik?
[Pa, what the hell is this? I told you already to stop. Can't you shut up for once?]

Lolo Carlos   Letseng batang 'to! Walang respeto! Parang hindi matanda ang kausap 'nyo!
[No respect! Who do you think you are, talking to your father like that!]

Tito Lenny   'Tay, nangako kayo na hindi na pag-uusapan ito! Kung alam ko lang na magwawala kayo, hindi na sana kita sinama! Putang ina mo!
[Pa, you promised you wouldn't do this! I never should have invited you here! Son of a bitch!]

Suddenly Lolo Carlos explodes, lunging at Tito Lenny and screaming curses in Tagalog.

Instantly, Roland is in the middle of the them, blocking Lolo Carlos from hitting Tito Lenny.

Roland   Tama na! Tama na 'yan! Enough!

Suddenly realizing this is happening in plain view of Ben, Rose and Gina, they stop. Still seething, Lolo Carlos' piercing glare tears into his sons.

Lolo Carlos   Mga suwail!
[Insolents!]

Lolo Carlos stomps off outside into the parking lot. Stunned, Roland takes a step back, goes around the corner, and turns to look inside the

Int. Gymnasium, bleachers – night, continuous

Silence as Ben and Rose stare back at their father. Humiliated, Roland looks down at the ground and shuffles away.

Gina is also looking down at the ground, eyes wet. Suddenly she looks up, grabs Ben's face and forces him to look at her as she finishes dressing his cuts. Time cut to

Ext. Parking lot, Rick's Mustang – night, continuous

Doug is sitting in the driver's seat of Rick's idling car, while Edwin, Jun and Rick hang out around him in a semi-circle. Mellow alternative rock is playing in the background on the car stereo.

Jun   Did you see the look on Ben's face? Dude was ready to go Cunanan.

Rick   What about his Pops? Now that was some loco shit.

Jun spots Ben walking up to them.

Jun   Ah, snaps! Ben!

Ben   Hey, guys.

They immediately surround him, patting him on the back, concerned.

Doug   Fuck, dude, you okay?

Ben   Yeah, yeah, I'm cool, I'm cool.

Rick   So what the fuck happened, man?

Ben   I don't know. Happened pretty fast. Just pissed me off, I guess.

Rick   Next time I see that G-Thing, I'm gonna drop kick his fuckin' ass.

Doug   Hello, Chuck Norris, the dude had a gun. *(to Ben)* You could've got your ass shot!

Jun   Damn, if I knew what he was carrying, I'd be off and running, Carl Lewis–style.

Ben chuckles, then grips his aching side.

Edwin	You sure you're okay, man?
Ben	I'm cool, just a little sore, that's all.
Rick	Yeah, Ben's a tough motherfucker.

Annabelle and Rose walk up behind them.

Rose	Hey, guys, Anna's gotta go.
Annabelle	Yeah, still got that curfew.
Edwin	Later, girl. Get some sleep.
Annabelle	Yeah, for a change.

Annabelle and Edwin exchange a friendly hug.

Jun	Hey, what about me?
Annabelle	Oh come here.

After Annabelle and Jun hug, she catches Ben looking at her. She looks down, embarrassed. An uncomfortable pause.

Rick	I guess that's our cue to roll.
Doug	Uh, yeah! You're sure you're gonna be all right, bro?
Ben	Definitely.
Edwin	You guys take it easy. Stay in school, don't do drugs.

Everyone laughs. Rick points at Edwin.

Rick	Man, you are a trip. *(to Ben)* We gotta hang out with this guy more often.
Edwin	Yeah, man, just give us a call. I'm always down for hanging with my brown brothers.

Edwin thrusts his fist in the air in a power salute.

Viva la Raza!

Rick does the power salute right back at Edwin.

Rick	Pilipino ako! *(beaming)* See, I know what's up with Pinoys.

They give each other a "People of Color Hug"—they clasp hands and hold, then hug and pat each other on the back at the same time.

Doug	Well, thank you for making me feel like such a honky.
Edwin	*(patting Doug on the back)* That's okay. It's not your fault.
	Doug and Rick pile into the car. Rick starts it up.
Ben	So I'll catch you guys on Monday?
Rick	Yeah. And don't forget, dude, you gotta hook me up with one of those barrel men.
Doug	Me too. And a giant fork and spoon.
	Everyone laughs as Doug and Rick drive off and honk their horn. Rose turns and hugs Annabelle.
Rose	Call me tomorrow, huh, girlfriend?
Annabelle	Sure.
	Rose taps Edwin and Jun on the shoulder and turns to leave.
Rose	See you inside, Ben.
Edwin	Uh, yeah, we're gonna go clean up.
	The guys smile suggestively at Ben as they follow Rose back to the gym, leaving them alone. An awkward moment.
Ben	So it's uh, a pretty dangerous area around here. May I walk you?
Annabelle	Yeah, sure. *(they start walking)* So, you've had a bummer of a night.
Ben	Yeah. But it was fun while it lasted, huh?
Annabelle	Yeah, it was. I'm sorry it ended up like this.
Ben	Like it's your fault. At least I learned how to cha-cha.
	Ben does a quick cha-cha step. Annabelle laughs.
Annabelle	I never got a chance to thank you for that drawing. That was really sweet of you.
Ben	Ah, it's no biggie.
Annabelle	I'm still trippin' on how you just clocked Gusto. I've never seen anybody do that before.
Ben	I don't know. It felt good at the time.

Annabelle	I don't think he's ever been to a party he didn't ruin.
Ben	I feel like an idiot. I should've just walked away.
Annabelle	That was classic Gusto for you. Always talking shit, looking for an excuse to act all hard.
Ben	Actually, I was just thinking maybe Augusto's right.
Annabelle	Right about what?
Ben	That I'm a sell out. A coconut.
Annabelle	Oh right. Like he should talk. When we first started going out, he used to braid his hair into cornrows.
Ben	*(laughing)* If you think that's bad, you should've seen me in junior high. I used to sleep with a clothespin on my nose to make it look more pointed. I think I wanted to look more like Jason Priestley or something.
Annabelle	Oh come on. You have a cute nose. *(she rubs his nose)* Flat noses are nice. They don't get all smashed up when you try to kiss somebody.

They are in front of Annabelle's car, a Toyota Tercel.

Ben	You know what? I think you need a back rub right now. It's been a long day.
Annabelle	Oh really? Are you sure your hands are big enough?

Annabelle and Ben place their hands together.

Ben	I think they'll do.

She gives him a peck on the cheek. Ben just looks at her, then pulls her to him and kisses her full on the lips, long, hard, and passionate.

They finally move apart. Ben smiles at Annabelle warmly, who looks absolutely knocked out.

Annabelle	Ah, yeah, well. Your sister has my, um, phone number. Call me. Let me know how you're…doing.
Ben	Sure. Bye.

Hold on Ben smiling happily as he watches her drive off. Dissolve to

Ext. Ben's neighborhood – night

Long shot of the Vincent Thomas Bridge. Its lights shimmer in the clear night sky. Dissolve to

Ext. Ben's bedroom – night

Montage of shots as Ben sits at his easel, drawing. He has a number of Tita Connie's Polaroids clipped to his sketch pad.

Close on the Polaroids. All the major moments from the evening are here—the Greeting Line, the Modern Dance, Roland's song.

Extreme close up on Ben's hand as it draws in the sketch pad. We can't see what his subject is.

Extreme close up on a paint brush as Ben applies red paint to the drawing.

Extreme close up on Ben's eyes, intent on his work.

The montage continues as Ben stays up all night, working on the painting. Close on Ben as he finishes, the light behind him slowly changing from night to day. Dissolve to

Int. Ben's bedroom – day, morning

Early morning sunlight peeks through the blinds, casting bands of orange light all around the room. Ben sits in bed with his portfolio open in his lap. Tita Connie's Polaroids of the party are scattered around him. He picks up one, scrutinizes it. Close on Ben as he stares at the snapshot, thinking.

Insert – Polaroid

The candid shot Tita Connie took of Ben, Roland and Lolo Carlos at their dinner table.

Ben looks up and outside his door to see

Int. Ben's door/hallway – day, continuous

Roland exiting his bedroom from down the hall. Dressed in old, worn pajamas, Ben's father looks haggard. Beaten.

Roland catches his son's gaze and…looks down at the floor. He rounds a corner, off frame.

Int. Ben's bedroom – day, continuous

Ben stares at the empty doorway a moment, then grabs his portfolio and leaves.

Int. Kitchen – day, continuous

Ben enters to find his dad at the stove frying up some rice with garlic. Roland doesn't turn around. Ben stands quietly for a long, awkward moment, staring at his slouched back.

Ben   You gave Sinatra a run for his money last night.

Roland grunts. A beat.

Tito Lenny was telling us about your singing days.

No response. Finally…

Roland   I was very young then.

Roland puts a plate of longanisa (Filipino breakfast sausage) in the microwave.

Ben   I wasn't planning on telling you this so soon, but… I withdrew all my savings. Paid off my first year's tuition at Cal Arts. I'm not taking that scholarship to UCLA. *(long beat, no reaction)* Well…aren't you gonna yell at me now or something?

Roland opens up a cabinet, takes out some salt, sprinkles it on the rice. A beat as he thinks.

Roland   All your savings?

Ben   Yeah. It took that, even with the loan I got from the school.

Roland   So much money, Ruben. For a hobby.

Ben walks up beside his dad, turns on the coffee maker and silently proceeds to make coffee. After he finally pours the water into the machine, he pulls out his portfolio and opens it.

Ben   This is my portfolio. Cal Arts accepted me on this.

Ben pages through it.

Insert – portfolio

It's an impressive collection of incredibly intricate and beautiful cartoon drawings with a broad range of styles and techniques.

I was just working on this.

Ben turns the sketch pad to a formal portrait of Lolo Carlos, Roland and Ben taken from Tita Connie's Polaroid.

Roland is speechless as he stares at the painting a long moment. The microwave beeps. Roland snaps out of his stupor and turns to remove the sausage.

The fried rice is starting to smoke on the stove. Ben turns off the heat.

Roland grunts and pushes a plate of longanisa towards Ben. Ben tentatively tries a bite, almost chokes.

Roland   Be careful, it's hot.

In the other room, the phone rings.

Well, I'm going to get ready for church. I'll talk to your Mom about this Cal Arts thing...

Roland turns to find Gina and Rose eavesdropping by the doorway.

Hoy! What are you doing? We're going to be late.

Roland exits, followed by Gina and Rose, who both smile warmly at Ben as they turn to leave.

Ben picks up a longanisa and starts to munch on it as we pull back and credits start to roll.

Fade out.

The End

Biographies

CAST

Gina Alajar (Gina)

Gina started her illustrious acting career in the Philippines at the age of eight, when she won the Best Child Actress award for her first film, *Ang Kaibigan Kong Santo Niño* (*My Friend the Christ Child*). In 1996 she won the FAMAS (Filipino Academy of Movie Arts and Sciences) Best Supporting Actress award for her role in the film *Mulanay*.

Bernadette Balagtas (Rose)

Featured in films such as Trimark's *Chairman of the Board*, Rysher Entertainment's *High School High* and James L. Brooks' award-winning *As Good As It Gets*, Bernadette Balagtas shines as Ben's beautiful and proud older sister. In addition to film and theater performances, she is active on the comedy circuit as a stand-up comedienne.

Danté Basco (Ben)

Danté Basco started the new millennium by signing a development deal with Fox for his own TV series. Famous for starring as Rufio in Steven Spielberg's *Hook*, he recently starred in the independent feature *But I'm a Cheerleader*

and the soon-to-be-released *Rave*. Danté has also
guest-starred on many television shows, including
Touched By An Angel, *Moesha*, and *Nash Bridges*.

Darion Basco (Augusto)

A gifted, rising star, Darion Basco starred recently in
hundred percent, a quirky Asian American comedy that
opened both the 1998 Chicago Asian American Showcase
and the Los Angeles Asian Pacific Film and Video Festival.
He has also played supporting roles in the feature film
version of *The Brady Bunch* as well as in numerous TV
series, including *ER*, *Chicago Hope*, and *Blossom*. Darion
recently completed MTV's *Camp P*, which was produced by
hip hop mogul Master P.

Derek Basco (Edwin)

Derek Basco, the eldest of the Basco Brothers, starred
recently with Tommy Davidson in *Pros & Cons*, out in
theaters soon. He can also be seen in the Harrison Ford film
6 Days, 7 Nights, *Sgt. Bilko*, and *Riot*, Showtime's critically
acclaimed film about the 1992 Los Angeles riots. Derek also
has recurring roles on three television shows—*Becker*
(starring Ted Danson), *Love and Money*, and *Sorority*, a new
MTV show.

Dion Basco (Rommel)

In addition to *the Debut*, Dion appeared alongside
Halle Berry and James Belushi in the Tri-Star feature film
Race the Sun. He has also had featured roles in the TV
shows *Chicago Hope* and *Sweet Surrender*, and can be seen
every Saturday morning on NBC's *City Guys*.

Joy Bisco (Annabelle)

Energetic newcomer Joy Bisco plays Ben's love interest and Rose's best friend. Extremely talented in dance and sports, she has co-starred in a number of TV shows, including *Diagnosis Murder*, *JAG*, and *Strangeluck*. She has also had roles in the television pilots *Bladesquad*, *All About Us*, *Blue Harvest*, and *The Best Club*.

Conrad Cimarra (Nestor)

A former member of the Tony award-winning San Francisco Mime Troupe, Conrad toured the country performing *Aspects*, a series of monologues on racism and multiculturalism. He has also recently turned in critically acclaimed performances as Mercutio in *Romeo and Juliet* and Trinculo in *The Tempest*.

Tirso Cruz III (Roland)

Tirso began his career as a successful singer and became a certified matinee idol throughout the '70s. He is best known for his various roles as popular Filipina actress Nora Aunor's leading man. Numerous awards and nominations have made him a much sought after actor.

DJ E-man and DJ Icy Ice (themselves)

DJ Icy Ice (Isaiah Dacio) and DJ E-man (Emmanual Coquia) are top-rated Filipino American DJ's at leading Los Angeles hip hop radio stations 92.3 The Beat and Power 106, respectively. Both perform weekly at Los Angeles' most popular night clubs, and E-man is Musical Director at Power 106.

Eddie Garcia (Lolo Carlos)

Versatile Eddie Garcia has been acting for the past forty-six years, and has received three Best Actor and six Best Supporting Actor awards from various award-giving bodies in the Philippines. He has also garnered much respect on the other side of the camera as a recipient of five FAMA awards (the Filipino equivalent of the Oscars) for Best Director. At the age of 78, he is considered the Gentleman of Filipino Cinema and is one of his country's most respected entertainers.

Nicole Hawkyard (Susie)

Nicole Hawkyard received her B.F.A. in Drama from the University of California, Irvine, where she acted in such plays as *Antigone* and *The Merchant of Venice*. She then moved to Los Angeles to pursue acting in film and television. In addition to *the Debut*, you can see her as Claire on MTV's *Undressed*.

Gina Honda (Tita Florie)

Gina was born in Manila, and holds a Bachelor's degree in Acting and Directing from Cal State Los Angeles. She has worked extensively in theatre, film, television, and radio, and has also produced and managed several shows for The Mark Taper Forum in Los Angeles, including works for their Asian Pacific American Friends of Center Theatre Group Reading Series. In 1994, she won a Virgo Award for Best Female Lead in the original stage play *Whispers of an Asian Bride*.

Kayamanan Ng Lahi

Celebrating its tenth anniversary this year, Kayamanan Ng Lahi is one of the most critically acclaimed Philippine dance troupes in the U.S. In addition to providing innovative educational programs and artistic presentations,

KNL has performed in countless shows and festivals and co-produced a play with East-West Players.

Fe de Los Reyes (Alice)

A beloved singer and stand up comedienne in the Philippines, Fe got her start in the revered Manila showband Music and Magic, which performed extensively throughout Asia and North America. *the Debut* marks her first appearance in an American feature film.

Emelina Moll (Tita Connie)

After raising her family, Emelita finally found some free time to take up her long ambition to act. In just four short years, she has performed in numerous plays, commercials, and TV shows. She starred recently in *Flipzoids* at the San Diego Asian American Repertory Theater. Emelita is also a licensed Holistic Health Practitioner and a massage therapist.

Premiere (themselves)

Sisters Gigi and Alisha Floresca and soul sister Leslye Maninang make up the hot R&B group, Premiere. Their first album, produced by Denzil Foster and Thomas McElroy (of En Vogue, Tony Toni Toné, and Madonna fame), generated several hit singles and an appearance on the television show *Soul Train*. *the Debut* marks their first film appearance.

Jayson Schaal (Doug)

Originally from Michigan, Jayson has quickly adapted to the pace of Hollywood. He has appeared in numerous TV movies and series, including the Fox pilot *Exposed* and the NBC series *The Fresh Prince of Bel Air*. In addition to *the Debut*, he has a feature film entitled *Wasted*. He is under contract with the Coca Cola Company, and is appearing in an ongoing series of commercials for Surge soda.

Mindy Spence (Jennifer)

Most recently, Mindy guest-starred on Fox TV's hit comedy *That 70's Show*, and the TNT feature film, *Hard Time*, with Burt Reynolds. She has also starred alongside Suzanne Somers in the movie *Seduced by Evil*, and with Shelley Long in the Fox pilot *Home*.

CREW

Hisham Abed (Director of Photography)

After graduating from the Film Production School at the University of Southern California in 1986, Abed traveled the world with the Welfare Association of Geneva, Switzerland and documented relief efforts in Israel, the West Bank, and Gaza before moving on to concentrate on live-action photography. Of Arab American descent, Abed's broad expanse of work includes award-winning and critically acclaimed feature films, documentaries, short films, music videos and commercials.

Gene Cajayon (Director, Co-Producer and Co-Writer)

Gene Cajayon was born in Saigon, Vietnam during the War to a Filipino father and a Vietnamese/French mother. As an infant he and his family immigrated to the United States, living first in Chicago and eventually settling in Orange County, California. Growing up with equal doses of Filipino, Vietnamese and American culture, he fell in love with movies at an early age, and hopes to continue producing films about Filipino and Asian American experiences. *the Debut* is his first feature film.

John Manal Castro (Co-Writer)

Hailing from San Jose, California, co-writer John Manal Castro's first foray into filmmaking occurred as a student at California State University, Long Beach where he produced, wrote and directed his acclaimed short film *Diary of a Gangsta Sucka*, a biting mockumentary satirizing the Filipino gangster phenomenon in suburban Los Angeles. The film has appeared in numerous venues, including public television, the International Channel, and various film festivals around the country. *the Debut* is his first feature-length script.

Pia Clemente (Line Producer)

A graduate of the American Film Institute, Pia is a veteran producer of numerous commercials and music videos. *the Debut* was Pia's first feature film as Line Producer. A Filipina American, she originally hails from New York City, and now resides in Hermosa Beach, California.

Patricio A. Ginelsa (Associate Producer)

Patricio grew up in Daly City, California, where he started making video movies with his neighbors at the age of thirteen. He graduated from Jefferson High School and received his B.A. in Cinema Production at the University of Southern California. Starting out as a production intern in 1997, Patricio worked his way up to Associate Producer of *the Debut*. Under Kid Heroes Productions, he continues to write and develop his own movie projects.

Kenn Kashima (Editor)

Kenn is a Japanese American from San Diego, California. He graduated from San Francisco State University with a B.A. in Film and a Minor in Asian American Studies. In addition to *the Debut*, his feature film credits include *Yellow*, *Matters of Consequence*, and *Looking for Bruce*. He has also edited extensively for television, and is currently working on UPN's *Blind Date*.

Lisa Onodera (Producer)

Lisa Onodera is a Japanese American independent producer best known for the 1995 film *Picture Bride*, which won the Audience Award at the 1995 Sundance Film Festival and was distributed by Miramax Films. She lives in Santa Monica with her husband Greg Spence and son Orson James Spence.

5 Card Productions
and
Celestial Pictures
present

in association with
National
Asian American
Telecommunications
Association
GMA Network Films
Visual Communications

the Debut

Directed by	Gene Cajayon
Produced by	Lisa Onodera
Written by	Gene Cajayon
	John Manal Castro
Executive Producer	Gene Cajayon
Associate Producers	John Manal Castro
	Lu Cien Hioe
	Patricio Ginelsa, Jr.
Director of Photography	Hisham Abed
Editor	Kenn Kashima

Cast
(in order of appearance)

Ben Mercado	Danté Basco
Doug	Jayson Schaal
Dave	Brian Card
Jennifer	Mindy Spence
Susie	Nicole Hawkyard
Rick	Brandon Martinez
Tito Lenny	Ernie Zarate
Gina Mercado	Gina Alajar
Tita Connie	Emelita Moll
Tita Florie	Gina Honda
Roland Mercado	Tirso Cruz III
Rose Mercado	Bernadette Balagtas
Jun	Rawlins Apilado
Edwin	Derek Basco
Annabelle	Joy Bisco
Tito Dante	Louie Gonzales
DJ Robbie Rock	Robbie Pagatpatan
DJ E-Man	Emmanuel Coquia
DJ Icy Ice	Isaiah Dacio
Photographer	Abe Pagtama

Videographer	Gabe Pagtama
Alice Johnson	Fe de Los Reyes
George Johnson	Roland Kerr
Augusto	Darion Basco
Rommel	Dion Basco
Nestor	Conrad Cimarra
Lolo Carlos	Eddie Garcia
Car Guy	Blas Lorenzo
Alisha	Alisha Floresca
GiGi	Gigi Floresca
Leslye	Leslye Maninang
Car Girl	Arianna Basco
Line Producer	Pia Clemente
Original Score Composed by	Wendell Yuponce
Philippine Dance and Music Performed by	Kayamanan Ng Lahi
	Philippine Folk Arts
Modern Dancers & Choreographers	Ira Amilhussin
	Kimberly Maniquis
	Rawlins Apilado
	Shannon Quon
	Joselito Neri
	Daisy Alcayaga
Co-Executive Producers	Dexter Adriano
	Salvatore Baldomar Sr.
	Renato & Francoise Cajayon
	Felizardo J. Carlos
	Processo S. Carlos
	Sherland Fuertez
	Maria Paz L. Mugol
	Jay Sanchez
	Roman Santos
	Greg Spence
	Gregory Williams
	The Viana Family
Costume Designer	Francis E. Ocon
Production Designer	Michael Rizzo
First Assistant Directors	Bill Berry
	Alex MacInnis
Second Assistant Director	Brad Arnold

Casting Directors	Anna Fishburn	Additional Camera	Blake Jackson
	Andrew Ooi	B Camera First	
	John Miyasaki	Assistant Camera	Winnie Huen
	Jojo Jacob	Loader Interns	Eric Green
	Victor Manalo		Marco Hoffman
Casting Associates	Belen Santos		
	Bogee Romero	Still Photographer	Shane Sato
	Christina de Haven		Roger Fojas
	Cynthia Solis		
	Gina Honda	Title Sequence	
	Glenda Sino-Cruz	Photography	Roger Fojas
	Greg Bacani	Gaffer	Sal Aridi
	Here and Now	Best Boy Electric	Aaron Knoke
	Jupiter Legaspi		
	Louie Gonzales	Electricians	Neil MacLean
	Ryan Suda		Douglas A. Cragoe
			Thomas Carey
Production			Lynda Cohen
Coordinator	Gloria Perretti		Tom Holm
			Dwight Lay
Production Secretary	Eileen J. Soriano	Key Grip	Jean-Pierre Marangakis
Assistant to		Best Boy Grip	Dave Nielsen
Mr. Cajayon	Christina de Haven		
		Grips	Geoffrey D. Knoller
Script Supervisor	Patrick Miller		Dave Nielsen
B Camera			William Sentelik
Script Supervisor	Amanda Horton		Mark Wright
			Anthony Michael Todd
Key Set			Bobby Moore
Production Assistant	Mark Estiandan		
		Title Sequence	
Production Assistants	Adam Gerlach	Producer	Jose Nuñez
	Nicholas Collins	Additional	
	Stacy Katzman	Production Design	Nathan Ogilvie
	Alex Lane		
	Russ Mezikofsky	Assistant	
	Kim Weaver	Production Design	Regina Acuña
	Phil Mariano		
	Nina Kunimoto	Set Decorator	Claudia Rebar
Location Manager	Nobuo Nakano	On Set Dresser	Augie Robles
Additional		Swing	Vince Brown
Location Manager	Minette Lew		
First Assistant Camera	Sunjay Kapoor	*"Why can't we fold the Last Supper in half?"*	
Second		Storyboard Artists	Patrick Gealogo
Assistant Camera	Brian G. Haigh		Christian de Castro
Steadicam &		Assistant Costumer	James K. Sy
B Camera Operator	Rafael Mueller		
Loader	Jeff Saladin	Key Makeup and Hair	"Tym" Shutchai Buacharern

Makeup and Hair Artists	Yvette Beebe		Edwin Realce
	Joni Running Bear		Derek Lucido
			Francine Antoinette Maigue
Additional Makeup and Hair Artists	Michele Lewis		Darin Malci
	Sharon Asamoto		Robbie Pagatpatan
	Kari Peterson		Raina Paquillo
	Jill Fehring-Kelley		Richard Paryno
	Lily Girning		Don Regua
	Rose Hlaing		Magnolia Sabalo
	Tien Tran		Ted Sarto
	Sandra Suarez		Jay Tapaoan
	Annalisa Talamayan		Servanda Teoxon
			Luis Teoxon
Sound Mixer	Matthew Nicolay		Matthew Tolentino
			Jonathan Ulibas
Boom Operator	Scott Doorley		Alberto Velasco
			Rachel Viana
Additional Production Sound	Curtis Choy		Robert Viana
Additional Boom	Alex Arai	Title Sequence Models	Stephen Amstutz
			Cameron Bender
			Natalie Casas

"Get me five extras…but not the Big Guy."

Background Talent	Jun Aglipay		Adam Driver
	Jeanne Aguinaldo		Jacqueline Felix
	David Austria		Glen Gilbert
	Rusheilla Aragay		Ginger Goldman
	Angelica Baladad		Susan Hebert
	Lovelynn Barlahan		Levi Holiman
	Irene Bayaca		Robin Miller
	Ronald Bayaca		Julian Nagle
	Grace Borrero		Andres Nuñez
	Joel Capellan		Christine Portillo
	Mike Coquia		Hilary Thompson
	Robyn de Jesus		Carolyn Tomei
	Ceferina de Haven		
	Marianne Decera	Physical Trainer	Janairo Hernandez
	Ken Ejan		
	Neil Estrada		
	Maria Eugenio		

"Too bad we can't have them dunk …"

	Robin Fajatin	Basketball Choreographer	Keith Gibbs
	Lawrence Fama	Stunt Coordinator	Michael R. Long
	Jean Paul Gamido		
	Jen Gaspar	Medic/Security	Production Security
	Jonathan Gaspar		
	Patricio Ginelsa, Jr.	Studio Teachers	Christine Miller
	Reginald B. Hernandez		Gloria de la Torres
	Robert Hilo		
	Francis Escano	Caterer	Chez Gourmet Cuisine
	Laryna	Craft Service	Lisa Weber
	Cathy Lorenzo		
		Accountant	RC Baral and Co.
			Howard Baral

125   the Debut

Production Legal	Pamela Kunath Law Offices of Bronson Bronson and McKinnon LLP		Artwork by	Shino Arihara Patrick Gealogo
			Negative Cutting	J and R Post
Additional Legal Assistance	David de Jesus Alan Brunswick Kolua Seiko		Color By	Fotokem
			Color Timer	Jim Williams
			Mixed In	Ultra-Stereo
Insurance Provided by	Disc Insurance		"Angels"	Arbel Espiritu

Production Legal — Pamela Kunath, Law Offices of Bronson, Bronson and McKinnon LLP

Additional Legal Assistance — David de Jesus, Alan Brunswick, Kolua Seiko

Insurance Provided by — Disc Insurance

Post Production Supervisior — Greg Spence

Post Production Assistant — John P. Raposas

Assistant Editor — Suzanne J. Hee

Additional Editor — Bernard Lhert

Music Supervisor — Kormann Roque

Assistant Music Supervisor — Arne Lucas

Additional Music Supervision — Jeff Chang

Sound Supervisor & Mixer — John M. Davis

Assistant Editor — Joe Leih

Post Production Sound Facility — Dackl Inc.

Foley — C-5

Foley Mixer — George Lara

Foley Artist — Marko Costanzo

Loop Group — Albert B. Sambat, Eduardo D. Sambat, Iris Ria Pacis, Erick Gonzales, Ron Ilano, Christina de Haven

Edited on an AVID Film Composer Provided By L.A. Digital Post Spectacle Entertainment — Sal Baldomar / Jack Santry

Animation Camera — Mar Elepaño

Visual Effects by — Van Ling

Artwork by — Shino Arihara, Patrick Gealogo

Negative Cutting — J and R Post

Color By — Fotokem

Color Timer — Jim Williams

Mixed In — Ultra-Stereo

"Angels" — Arbel Espiritu, Auxiliary to APPA, C.O. Semense, M.D., CSULB PAC, Dean Devlin, Dr. Pantaleon de Jesus, Dr. Ramon S. Quesada, Jr., FIND 2000, Gerald Reyes, Ilene Rockman, Larry Natividad, Melinda V. Reyes, Royal F. Morales, Noel Christian Price, Ernesto & Rosita Galang, Romeo & Delia Intia, Perry & Dolores Diaz, Philippine Medical Association of Michigan, Bangar Contractor's Corporation, Pilipino Cultural Exchange, Cal Poly SLO, PMA of Metro Washington, D.C., Ruben T. Briones, P.E.

Screenplay Advisors — Abraham Ferrer, Alex MacInnis, Brian Kandler, Chris Chan Lee, Chris Donohue, Clifford Son, Daniel Gonzales, Daniel Tirtiawinata, Dean Devlin, Dr. Santiago Sia, Ed Marsh, Eric Koyanagi, Fred Cheng, Howard Lavick, Jason Yamamoto, Joan Wai

Joe Virata
Johnny Garcia
Ken Ejan
Linda Mabalot
Mabel Orogo Cajayon
Mark Vincent Escaler
Myla Orogo
Natalie Rothenberg
The Insiders System for
Writers
Radmar Agana Jao
Russell Leong
Uncle Roy Morales

Howard Cabalfin
John P. Raposas
Karen Pagtama
Kristine Soto
Mariciel C. Basallo
Mark Estiandan
Michael Montecillo
Michelle "Mee-Shelle" Bicera
Nina Bautista
Oliver del Rosario Quirante
Sachi Cunningham
Steven Togami
Theresa Pedrena

Folks Who Let John and Gene Crash At Their Pads While They Wrote the Screenplay

Jeanne Aguinaldo
Johnny Garcia
Jojo Gonzalez
Joy Tiu
Ken Ejan
Ron Villena
Ryan Callo
The Braza Family
The Cajayon Family
The Castro Family
Theresa Castro & Bod Boyle
Zenus Balbuena

Editorial Advisors

A.J. Calomay
Alex MacInnis
Chamina Maniquis
Edgar Dormitorio
Greg Spence
Howard Lavick
John Manal Castro
LMU Isang Bansa
Lu Cien Hioe
PAMANA of South H.S.
Pia Clemente
Ugnayan of Leuzinger H.S.
Walt Louie

Interns & Volunteers

A.J. Calomay
Carlyle Rafanan
Christian de Castro
Christina de Haven
Christine Anne Mendoza
Conrad Viana
Don Deleon
Genevieve Sagun
Glenda Sino-Cruz

Music Consultants

A.J. Calomay
Chie Orogo
Christine Anne Mendoza
Conrad Viana
Genevieve Sagun
John Manal Castro
John P. Raposas
Mabel Orogo Cajayon
Mariciel C. Basallo
Michael Montecillo
Michelle "Mee-Shell" Bicera
Nina Bautista
Oliver del Rosario Quirante
Patricio Ginelsa, Jr.

Fridge Provided By Winston "Ton Ton" Emano

"Tomato Kid"
Written by T. de Pala
E. Encarnacion
K. Encarnacion
G. Salgado
Performed by Moonpools and Caterpillars
Courtesy of MCA Universal/
Polygram Records

"Jota Angelina"
Written by Nitoy Gonzales
Performed by Kayamanan Ng Lahi
Philippine Folk Arts

"Ikaw"
Written by M. Velarde Jr.
D. Santiago
Performed by Tirso Cruz III

"World People"
Written by Duran
Pangan
Performed by Native Elements
Produced by Native Elements
Co-Produced by Ralston Grant
Courtesy of Native Elements

"Talkin' 2 U"
Written by K. Osorio
Jean-Yves G. Ducornet
Additional Lyrics by Rodney Hidalgo
Eric Cruz
Richmond Andal
Performed by Devotion
Produced by Jeeve for Where's
My Cut Productions
Courtesy of Jamboe Entertainment

"Come See Us"
Written by G. Chacon
A. Oregana
P. Sirate
San Quinn
Performed by KNT featuring San Quinn
Courtesy of 20/20 Records/
Classified Records, Inc.

"Peach Durango"
Courtesy of Killer Tracks

"Invasion of the
Octopus People"
Produced, Written,
& Composed by DJ QBert
Published by Reverse Cat
Breath Publishing
Courtesy of Galactic Butt Hair Records

"Won't Last"
Written by C. Jones
Performed by C.O.
Produced by Phishbone
Courtesy of ILLFA MUZK

"Backflip
(Phishbone Remix)"
Written by J. Merchan
Performed by BIGG KNUTT FUNK
Featuring Puff
Produced by Phishbone
Courtesy of ILLFA MUZK

"Raw"
Written by G. Chacon
A. Oregana
P. Sirate
San Quinn
Performed by KNT Featuring San Quinn
Produced by Mr. Sirate
Courtesy of 20/20 Records/
Classified Records, Inc.

"Strum"
Written by Aurelius Goldie Masaoy
Ryan Paayas
Performed by Basement 31
Courtesy of Basement Soundz

"Old Man"
Written by Jeremiah Delino
Performed by The Speaks
Courtesy of Toledo Productions, Inc.

"Intro to Magic"
Written by G. Mungcal
Performed by Silverscene
Courtesy of p-noize records

"Amenece en Isla Verde"
Courtesy of Killer Tracks

"Swing Thing"
Courtesy of Killer Tracks

"I Need to Know"
Written by E. Visperas
R. Brown
Performed by Innerlude
Produced by Ricky "R&B" Brown For
Big Rick Productions
Courtesy of Straight Hits

"Singkil"

Folkloric Composition
Performed by Kayamanan Ng Lahi
Philippine Folk Arts

"Love Nest #1"
Written by J. Mason
Performed by Johnson
Produced by Johnson
Courtesy of TODADEF Music

"Everyone"
Written by J. Mason
Performed by M. O. F.
Produced by Johnson
Courtesy of TODADEF Music

"Roscoe's CNW"
Written by Roscoe Umali
Performed &
Produced by Kooya Roscoe Umali
Featuring Aristotle
Published by Sumo Publishing
Courtesy of Sumo Records

"Time Won't Wait"
Written by F. Valle
J. Rojo
A. Lucas
H. Felina
P. Sirate
Performed by IF Featuring P-Kid
Produced by IF
Courtesy of ILLFA MUZK

"Rack Em Up"
Written by J. Mason
Performed by Johnson
Produced by Johnson
Courtesy of TODADEF Music

"Just…"
Words by Melissa Fuentefria
Ryan Paayas
Performed by Basement 31
Courtesy of Basement Soundz

"Ladies"
Written by J.P. Nebres
Performed by DNH
Produced by J.P. Nebres for
Beat Digga Productions
Courtesy of Classified Records, Inc.

"Set It"
Written by M. Taba
R. Balbarin
R Quijano
Performed by Pacifics

"Agent Orange"
Written by Jamir Garcia
Performed by Slapshock
Courtesy of Virgin/OctoArts/EMI
Music Inc.

"Quit Stressin'
(Rock Steelo Remix)"
Written by S. Alexander
Performed by Ora
Produced by Sean Alexander
Courtesy of Blacklisted 4 Lyfe
Entertainment Inc.

"Is It Real"
Written by J.P. Nebres
A. Abiog
M. Briones
L. Reyes
Performed by Pinay
Produced by J.P. Nebres for
Beat Digga Productions
Courtesy of Classified Records, Inc.

"My Friend"
Written by D. Seegmiller
Performed by DNH
Produced by Darwin Seegmiller
Kormann Roque
Courtesy of Classified Records, Inc.

	"Martians"		The Orogo Family
Written by	T. de Pala		The Pagtama Family
	E. Encarnacion	Celestial Pictures	Michael & Tonia Hsieh
	K. Encarnacion		Peter Shiao
	G. Salgado		Bryan Oh
Performed by	Moonpools and Caterpillars		Juli Kang
Courtesy of	MCA/Universal/		Suzan Wang
	Polygram Records		Taemi Lim
			Wei Koh
	"Southern Dreamer"		
Written by	Emm Gryner		Fritz Friedman
Performed by	Emm Gryner		Ernest Escaler
Courtesy of	Dead Daisy Records		Christopher Lee

"Should that big fork and spoon be crooked?"

	"I'm Sayin' Though"		
Written by	P. Sirate	NAATA	Janice Sakamoto
	K. Gabbert		Deann Borshay
	S. Roybal		Eddie Wong
Performed by	Mr. Sirate		Charles Kim
	Ken Swift	Visual	
	Zulu Gremlin	Communications	Jerome Academia
Additional Vocals by	Annalisa De Lena		Callie Chung
Scratches by	Marvin Mister Sison		John Esaki
Produced by	Mr. Sirate		Abraham Ferrer
Courtesy of	Mr. Sirate and Zulu Gremlin		Kennedy Kabasares
			Amy Kato
	"Devoted"		Chil Kong
Written by	M. De Leon		Walt Louie
	T. Nicolas		Linda Mabalot
Performed by	Julie Plug		Cheryl Yoshioka
Produced by	Elvin M. Reyes	GMA Network Films	Butch Jimenez
Courtesy of	Classified Records, Inc.	Centropolis	
		Entertainment	Dean Devlin
	"You're the One For Me		Tavin Marin-Titus
	(Remix)"		Deionne McNeff
Written by	Freda Simone		Peter Winther
Performed by	Freda Simone		Kim Winther
	Featuring Grand Vanacular	Lightstorm	
Scratches by	D.J. Icy Ice of the	Entertainment	
	World Famous Beat Junkies	Production	
Courtesy of	IQ Entertainment	Department	Geoff Burdick
Grand Vanacular			Al Rives
courtesy of	Suburban Noise		Mike Trainotti
Extra Special Thanks To	The Baldomar Family	Cantwell Sacred	
	The Cajayon Family	Heart of Mary H.S.	Principal David Chambers
	The Castro Family		Zavan Hadjinian
	The Felix Family		Tony Guggino
	The Floresca Family		
	The Maninang Family		
	The Nuñez Family		

Saints Peter and Paul
Catholic Church

City of Montebello

Loyola Marymount
University   Howard Lavick
Ian Conner
John Stewart
Rick Hadley
LMU Calendar Office
LMU APSS
Eric Kohatsu
Joe Virata
Dr. Santiago Sia

CSU Long Beach   Dr. Jose Sanchez-H.
John Caldwell

Apple Computer   Doug Werner

iJeepney.com   Winston "You Know Who's
Filipino" Emano
Avelino J. Halagao

Filipinas Magazine
Philippine News
Los Angeles Asian Journal

Cebu Performing
Arts Foundation

Chris Ramos
Mai-Ling Andreen
NIPA

Louie Gonzales &
Kuh Ledesma

pinoynet.com/
pinoymall.com   Eric Ilustrisimo
Ramses Reynoso
Neil Romero

Asian American
Theater Company
Guy Lee
East-West Players
PAHA
Manila Actors Studio
Chris Ramos

*"Why do you have to party over here
when there's a party over there?"*

Legend Entertainment

The 21XL
Events Company   David Gonzalez
Tien Tran

Festival of Philippine
Arts & Culture

Long Beach
Filipino Artists Guild

Albert Morti

Search to Involve
Pilipino Americans (SIPA)

CSULA Hiyas
CSULB Kappa Phi Epsilon
CSULB Pilipino
American Coalition

El Camino College Maharlika
PAC Modern
SCPASA
UCI Kababayan
UCLA Samahang Pilipino

Team Flux
Yosi-Drag
Rush Factor
Mason Tolentino
Ruel Sangco
Alan Cajayon
June Fueconcillo

Cyber Java   Rom Augustin
Danilo Garing

Killer Tracks   Caroline Mansoury,
"The Sales Diva"

"Are we filming the Lechon Guys today?"

A.J. Calomay & Bahay Bidyo
Alex and Gayle Cardenas
Annie Imhoff
Auntie Irene Sumi
Becky Tan & Point Point
Joint Restaurant
Casey Cannon
Chi Zee
Chris Donohue
Christopher Tarroza
Edwin Habacon &
Tribal Pinoy
Eliza Escaño
Emil Soriano

Estrella Chan
Genie Fernandez
Howard Cabalfin
Irene Soriano
Jeanne Aguinaldo
Joel Tan
Jun E. Hingco
Kid Heroes Productions
Leslie Macabeo
Lorna Halili &
Manila Sunset Restaurant
Mark Pulido
Moonie Lantion &
pinoylife.com
Rosa Zee
Van Go's Ear
Van Partible
Wade Wisinski

"John, I'm getting married …"

"Debut"
Fundraising Trailer   Chris Asano
Chris Davis
Christopher Crook
David Chameides
Eric Walters
Hedda Solloest
Jaime Martin
Jenn Malchiodi
Joe Braza
Justin Stolo
Maria Hanson
Michelle Pederson
Muni Zano
Paul Fisher
Radmar Agana Jao
Rena Heinrich
Richard Chen
Sherland Fuertez
Sierra Knolle

Stress Relief   3 AM Sportscenter
March Madness
Missile Command
NBA
Olde English 800
Thai Charcoal Pit
Vivid Video

Gene's Therapist   Dr. Paul Fisher

…and to everyone else who helped out and were down for the Brown—Much Mahal!

No animals were harmed during the making of this film…except for those three lechons.

The characters and events depicted in this photoplay are fictitious. Any similarity to actual persons, living or dead, is purely coincidental. This film is a work of fiction and does not represent the actions or beliefs of a particular culture or religion.

Ownership of this motion picture is protected by copyright and other applicable laws and any unauthorized duplicating, distribution, or exhibition of this motion picture could result in criminal prosecution as well as civil liability.

"So you likes?"

debutfilm.com

for all the children who made their debut during production…

aidan
alexandra
brianna
everett
kai
kaimali'okeao
malaya
orson
tala
theophilus
vincent
will